# THE
# BOOK OF JUJU

# THE
# BOOK OF JUJU

## AFRICANA SPIRITUALITY FOR HEALING, LIBERATION, AND SELF-DISCOVERY

## JUJU BAE

STERLING ETHOS
New York

STERLING ETHOS
New York

ISBN 978-1-4549-5128-5
ISBN 978-1-4549-5129-2 (e-book)

Library of Congress Control Number: 2023949813

For information about custom editions, special sales, and premium purchases, please contact
specialsales@unionsquareandco.com.

Printed in the United States of America

2 4 6 8 10 9 7 5 3 1

unionsquareandco.com

Cover and interior design by Gavin Motnyk
Cover illustration by Diana Ejaita
Images by Shutterstock.com: Sidhe: 114; Joe Stickman: 96, 97

I often feel sad when I think about your leaving me while in the middle of writing this book, but then I remember that you left so that you could join me. This book is for you, my grandmommy Dr. Ellestine J. Grant.

# CONTENTS

# THE BEGINNING

When people ask me, "When did you start your spiritual journey?" I feel the multiple paths I've walked in my life illuminating. Even as a child, I knew that Spirit existed. Concepts like God, saints, spirituality, ceremony, ritual, and even ancestors were always present in my forms of worship, whether I was in the church or in the Bahá'í temple. I remember praying to God that my grandmother's car would start up again when it broke down outside the house—and it did. I remember being eight years old and intuitively laying my hands on my best friend's stomach when she had a bellyache, and her exclaiming, "Wow, that worked!" Whether it was my African naming ceremony as a baby, facilitated by my Aunt Myrtle, or my chats to my pop-pop after he passed, I knew something bigger was there for me. As far as I can tell, my spiritual journey existed before I even had the language to describe it as such. My journey has always lived alongside me.

Allendale and Edmondson Avenue is where I received my introduction to what it means to be a devout worshiper, an intentional prayer, and a ritualized Black human. My experience as a good Black Catholic girl started in a large gray brick building under a gold dome that would sparkle in the sun as if the Holy Spirit herself had pursed her lips to kiss it. St. Bernadine's Roman Catholic Church, the all-Black congregation perpetually led by a white head priest, was located in the Southwest Baltimore, Maryland, community of Edmondson Village. The big gray brick seemed to tower over the brown row homes and my little brown body as my father and I entered the side door, nearest the corner store, every Sunday morning around 11ish. St. Bernadine's, my Black Catholic haven, gave everyone the Roman Catholic aesthetic that we came for: beautiful stained-glass windows and lingering scents of frankincense and myrrh welcomed devoted adults and bored children alike. Eventually the white Jesus paintings that graced the walls were repainted to a dark-skinned man with locs, to better mirror the parishioners who filled the church in this all-Black neighborhood. Now, St. Bernadine's was not the church where I nonconsensually accepted the teachings of the Catholic Church to wash me of the sins that I was apparently born with as an infant—better known as baptized—but it *is* the church that I attended for over ten years of Christmas concerts and early Mass until I decided that I wanted to be Baptist, and later Buddhist, then Bahá'í, and then a witch. It is where I learned that reciting the same prayers was basically chanting, and that body posture matters when addressing the Spirit (stand, sit, kneel, repeat). St. Bernadine's Roman Catholic Church was where my "Black church" experience began.

Believe it or not, Baltimore has quite the active Black Catholic community. If you're unfamiliar with my culturally unique hometown, Baltimore has the fifth largest population of African Americans in the United States. As seen in our crab cracking and our dirt bikes that are hardly ridden in dirt, Black culture is fully infused into what defines Baltimore—even the Roman Catholics. Of course, Baltimore is no New Orleans, Louisiana. We don't have as many Catholic schools, churches, or overall Catholic cultural imprint as does New Orleans. But we Baltimoreans have quite the expansive history of "firsts" regarding Catholic roots in the United States. In 1789, Pope Pius VI appointed Father John Carroll of Upper Marlboro, Maryland, the first Catholic bishop in the United States and selected Baltimore as the seat of the first diocese, which is basically a church district that is overseen by a bishop. This is like Baltimore being the first "state" in the Catholic world, followed by New Orleans in 1793. Baltimore is also home to the Oblate Sisters of Providence, who are the most successful Roman Catholic sisterhood in the world established by women of African descent. In 1829 these primarily Haitian Caribbean nuns founded a school for Black Catholic girls, which became the foundation of St. Frances Academy, the oldest continuously operating school for Black Catholic children in the United States. St. Frances Academy remains an active Catholic school in Baltimore today. Baltimore could never be left out of the conversation of Catholicism, and this conversation was my reality until I turned eighteen.

I attended Catholic school from kindergarten to twelfth grade. I was very well versed in what it meant to confess my sins to a priest, use prayer beads to set my intentions, and celebrate a bunch of "elevated" dead people, or saints, by leaving them offerings and prayers on "feast days." Sex outside marriage was sinful, being gay wasn't discussed, masturbating was selfish, and the behavior of some local priests was questionable at best. I went to Mass during school, received grades in religion classes, and prayed all the time. Faith was a big portion of my childhood identity. Even as a child I lived and breathed every ritual as if my life depended on it, because my soul *did*. I never considered that there could be more to my existence outside Catholicism until about eighth grade, when it was time for Confirmation. If you're unfamiliar with Catholic rites, at around fourteen years old, most good Catholic children move forward with the ceremony of Confirmation, which "confirms" your belief in the Catholic teachings and means that you fully accept Jesus as your savior. Catholic children are typically baptized as infants, so confirmation is our somewhat consensual choice into this faith. You go to classes to prepare for Confirmation, may have some additional praying, and even get to choose a new Catholic name for yourself after one of the saints! I believe mine was going to be Beatrice, or maybe it was Maria. But as my friends prepared for their Confirmation, picked out their Confirmation names, and their parents bought new white dresses or black suits for the ceremony, I decided that I didn't want to go through with this particular rite. Even as a preteen, something inside me decided that I didn't want to confirm my belief in the Catholic teachings. I did still identify as a Catholic, but I felt that if I was confirming something, then I should be sure, right? I was only fourteen, so I didn't feel like I could confirm anything besides what I was wearing on our out-of-uniform day at the school dance. Now, as an adult, I understand this as my *Ori* (higher consciousness) always guiding me to the traditions that felt safest and most comfortable, even if I didn't realize that yet. This was my first step in rejecting the status quo and the expectations surrounding my spiritual identity. At fourteen years old, I knew that there was more to my spiritual life than what I'd experienced so far.

Now, although I was a Catholic child baptized, churched, and schooled under the tenets of the Roman Catholic Church, I was blessed to have spiritual interactions with family and friends that consisted of a cocktail of Christianity. My paternal grandmother, with whom I spent much of my childhood in Edmondson Village, was born and raised Pentecostal—Holiness, to be exact. She later converted to African Methodist Episcopal (AME). Then there was my mother's side of the family, which was originally Baptist. My best friend, Alex, was also Baptist, and her church eventually became my church home. She lived right up the street from me in Southwest Baltimore, and as an only child I often favored her and her sister's company more than just my own. My father and my granddaddy, who gave me my Alabaman and Caribbean ancestry, were devout Catholics. My father directed the choir at St. Bernadine's and often played the bongos, too, while my mom was a quieter Catholic who eventually left the Church while I was in middle school. My mom remarried my "bonus" dad, whom I have never known as religious but was definitely spiritual in many senses, which I credit to his Louisianian and Chattanoogan roots. My maternal grandmother converted to Lutheran, and I'm not sure I ever saw her husband, my pop-pop, step foot in a church for anything beyond the major events such as baptisms or funerals. One of the paternal family churches is AME, while the other paternal side is Pentecostal from South Carolina, which I used to visit every summer growing up. So, if you can't tell, I've been churched all the way around. I've sat in every kind of Christian denomination setting you can imagine. And although I no longer identify with any of these labels, there's a strange way that Spirit moved in these spaces that prepared me to be the bad bitch witch Hoodoo Orisha juju lady that I am today. It's funny how Spirit moves.

The thing about Catholicism is that, once you leave, you see how ritualized, ceremonial, and "witchy" it really is (don't tell them I said that). I didn't learn about candle magic from a Wiccan lady or a New Age spiritualist on YouTube; I learned it, at least initially, from the Catholic Church. The concept of honoring deities and reaching out to "the dead" to intercede on my behalf was something I learned from Catholicism. To this day, Saint Anthony, the patron saint of lost items, was (and still is) one of the first spirits that I call on to help me find my wallet or missing cowrie earrings. I often wonder how and why he still blesses my non-Christian ass. The ideas of the supreme "Mother"—in other words, concepts of divine femininity and healing through the maternal—that I've come to understand within African diasporic spiritual systems were shown to me *first* through the exaltation of Jesus's mother, Mary, to whom we prayed on a spiritual necklace of sorts that the Catholics call a rosary.

You see, Catholics taught me about ritual. Holiness folks taught me how to shout and to "see" beyond my physical eyes. Pentecostals taught me how to dress and move before the Spirit. Baptists taught me how to pull out a spirit through a song and a hand clap. The Lutherans taught me reverence and to be still, but Catholics taught me how to hide in plain sight. Catholics taught me how to feed the spirits. Catholics informed me of the beginnings of how to be a witch.

I must note, however, that Catholicism has quite the messy and traumatic past and present. In many ways this religion in particular has been an embarrassment to Christians and non-Christians all over the world. Catholicism's relationship to plagiarism, rape, human trafficking, colonialism, and the theft of ancient African religion is still an undercurrent of its horrible history and active present. I think this amalgamation of spiritual trauma has informed much of my own spiritual, physical, and emotional trauma. I was a child immersed in the confusing world of what it meant to be a little Black Catholic girl—who also thinks she likes girls—in an extremely historic location for Catholic history. The abuse I witnessed as a child quite literally touched my family, teachers, and classmates, as people that I loved and knew were survivors of Catholic guilt, shame, and sexual trauma at the hands of pedophilic priests. Catholicism, with its layered functions, is a big part of why it's hard for me to trust my own elders, spiritual community, and sometimes even my own ancestors. It is part of how I know that religious spaces, regardless of denomination, can be breeding grounds for violence. However, this same violence that I witnessed taught me how to be a good spiritual practitioner. It taught me the value of protecting oneself spiritually and physically. And perhaps that protection is not always from some large unexplainable force like a devil, but from those who purport to be the angels in your own spiritual communities. It showed me that what we deem evil can thrive when it is backed by communities, political powers, and intentional prayers. It was my first true understanding of spiritual warfare, and the amount of control religious leaders hold throughout the entire world. Catholicism taught me that not every ritual is good, not every word is sacred, and not every spiritual house will be your home.

I was not only raised Catholic, but I attended Catholic school from kindergarten all the way to twelfth grade. In that process you can only imagine the level of harmful rhetoric I learned at the hands of well-meaning Catholic teachers. Of course there were the cool nuns who knew that you were having sex, drinking, and all the other teenage tales, but specifically in my Catholic middle school I internalized a lot of guilt surrounding pleasure, specifically masturbation. One day in class, this elderly-ass white couple came in and talked to us about the body and why it was sinful to have sex before marriage. This happened around eighth grade, so by that point I knew that sex was something to "wait for," although I'm not sure I actually planned on that. But during their presentation someone asked, "What about masturbation?" and the response was, "Well that's just absolutely selfish, and God doesn't like that, either." For some reason, this particular comment still resounds in my head at the most inconvenient times. The thought that self-pleasure is also something that is evil and selfish and could land you a first-class ticket to hell replays in my mind to this day. The imprint of that moment lasted for quite some time as I navigated my own sexuality and sought to discover what my body craved for and enjoyed. I've done a lot of sexuality and sensuality unlearning with my ancestors, because I never had space for that within my other belief systems. Remember, I was born with the right to experience joy and so were you, and that knowledge changed my relationship to my body and my identity.

Seeing and venerating ancestors has done a number not just on my sensual self, but on my self-confidence. I have a tattoo on my shoulder that I got many years ago while I was Christian to support me in having more confidence. The tattoo is trusty Proverbs 31:30 (LOL), and it reads, "Beauty is Vain." Although I understand why I felt that I needed that tattoo at that time in my life, I wish I had simply read that Bible verse every morning instead of tattooing it on my clavicle, because these days I do not share those sentiments at *all*. Beauty is not vain, and I know that because I have beautiful ancestors. And we don't have to be what we are told is beautiful to embody it. The way that my ancestors love, nurture, and care for me is beautiful. There was a point when I didn't like my dark skin, big forehead, or big eyes, but now that I root those traits in those of an ancestor of mine, I can see my own beauty. How dare I call myself ugly! My grandma ain't ugly. And whenever I see images of the faces of my ancestors in my mind, I know that my ancestors ain't ugly, either. The reverence that I carry for my departed loved ones has to extend to myself, because I am literally a reflection of them. If I wouldn't say it to a great-grandmother, I don't need to be saying it to me. Beauty is not vain—and if it is, what's wrong with vanity?

If you've come to this book today, welcome. Maybe you've come because you, like me, were indoctrinated under a system that didn't work for you, but you always knew there was more to the story than what you were being told. Perhaps you're deep into an African or African Diasporic Tradition but seeking to ground yourself in what brought you to that tradition. Perhaps you're curious about what Hoodoo is or are still trying to understand who the Orisha are and what place they may have in your life. Maybe you don't know, but you felt the tug to go deeper and to look no further than into your own spirit to connect with something divine. Regardless of what unique reasoning you have, may this be a balm on your journey.

The beginning chapters of this book cover definitions: who the ancestors are, why they are important, and other historical examples regarding the importance of ancestral veneration and the process of returning to Africana spiritual systems as Black people. This aspect of spirituality is vast, and developing some kind of grounding in it is important before we move on to the next section. In the latter parts of the book, we'll discuss the mechanics or the "how to" of engaging in these traditions. We'll cover concepts such as altar building, spirit communication, spiritual gifts, and rituals. I realize that everyone is always excited to jump into the rituals first, but please take time to process the historical and cultural information this book includes, too. It'll make your juju pop even more! On top of that, I'll provide questions, exercises, and journal prompts so that you can take note of what you're experiencing as you absorb this text, to work that third eye and get into habits of better ritual for yourself. I'll also be sharing personal stories about my spiritual journey, along with the ancestral tea that my spirits have been sharing with me throughout the past few years.

Whatever your reason for picking up this book, you've felt *something* calling you home to yourself and to your people . . . and all I can say is that if you've taken that first step, then you've already done the hardest part: listening. I encourage you to keep listening throughout this book, take notes on what comes up for you, and stay open to the transformative powers of our ancestral voices. I'm excited for you!

# CHAPTER 1

# ANSWERING THE CALL

Every single person is called to their ancestors or ancestral practices in some way. Although not everyone is a psychic, conjure person, or priest, the ancestors move in all our lives and seek to grow closer to us through the ways that work with each individual person. Everyday communion is a conversation with Spirit. When the wind blows, it is Spirit activating us and telling a story about the atmosphere in that moment. The waxing and waning of the moon is a story based on ancestral knowledge that has been passed down from ancient times that allows us to understand what actions are more or less beneficial during each phase. All of it is Spirit.

At this point, I've accepted the calling. If you're here, I'd bet that your ancestors have similar kinds of expectations of you. And you seem to have already listened to the calling in some way, just by opening a book like this! Congratulations: listening looks good on y'all. But I had no choice: by writing this book, I am obliging the directives of my own ancestors. And beyond that, I've learned way too much on my journey as a spiritualist not to share what has worked for me. The knowledge I'm sharing here is what encouraged me to be active in spiritual social media groups in the beginning of my juju journey, starting with my show, *A Little Juju Podcast*, that uplifts African and African-derived spiritual systems for Black people. This written offering is my own form of veneration and an archive of my personal and collective ancestral information. Their advice informs much of my own understanding of the world, its norms, and what we think are norms but are actually just a bunch of bullshit. As many ancient religions teach us, proper ancestral veneration and communication is the anchor to a well-adjusted and high-functioning society. Now I, as an American-born Black person, would argue: we ain't in that at all. The levels of violence, lack of community, extreme poverty, anti-Blackness, and anti-indigeneity we are currently experiencing as a society anchored in Western culture are indications of severe spiritual deprivation. This is not our fault, as so many of us are still trying to find our way, both as individuals and as a collective. But we have lost so many of the names of the deities who have historically protected us. We have been shunned from belief systems that encourage us to fight back and instead are told to turn the other cheek. We've been trained to value individualism instead of the power of the collective. We have been taught that, once our people are dead, they are just dead, and we have completely lost the power to connect or hear from them ever again—a lie. We have been taught that our ancient forms of Black-ass spirituality, veneration, and medicine making were all "bad juju" seeking to destroy our relationship to a one true God who would throw us in hell for having these beliefs. Another lie. This is a deliberate war on our spirits and an intentional severance of the power of our collective ancestors. That severance from our spiritual medicine has done significant damage to the psyche.

I call myself Juju or Juju Bae very intentionally. If you are unfamiliar with the term *juju*, it is often used to undermine and demonize the practice of African-based religious practices. Colloquially juju is understood as "bad" and "evil" magic conjured by ugly witches who seek to harm and even kill people through the use of spellwork and other demonic supernatural forces. Juju can also be used to describe a form of magic that can control individuals, leaving them powerless and unable to do anything but submit to the control of whatever the "witch" chooses. What's funny about this definition is that I don't totally disagree. I think folks throughout the African diaspora either know or know of a story about someone who succumbed to the powers of a witch and suffered greatly for it. There are stories of intense curses that have ruined families, and stories about men being bound to their partners nonconsensually because they were under a spell. All this and more is true. Juju can render harm, because juju is an acknowledgment that each of us has the ability and power to control certain outcomes in our lives. However, the misrepresentation of juju presents itself through the inaccurate representation that juju is *all bad*. Juju is not bad or good; it just is. The juju itself is actually a neutral force, whose use is at the discretion of the practitioner using it. In the same ways that juju has cursed family lines, that same juju has protected tribes, saved relationships, healed the sick, blessed homes, increased money flow, and welcomed babies into the world. Juju is our ancestral medicine, and only through the interruption of colonialism and Abrahamic tradition did we come to see juju as being inherently malevolent and against God.

I use the term *juju* to embrace our ancestral understandings of duality (which we will investigate through this book), and to help make sure that the concept of juju is accurately represented in the media. Hollywood depictions of Voodoo and similar traditions have tainted the way Black folks engage with the practices that helped heal their ancestors—through harmful stereotypes and a bunch of bullshit lies. I want to situate juju as something that is not only a vision of evil, but one of hope, freedom, healing, and love, *because it is*.

The Bae portion of my name is a nod to the Black American colloquial pet name that's short for *baby* and can refer to someone you like or love. It's an aspect of being cute, likable, and even fine, sexy, and fun. I think juju can be all those things, and that practitioners of these traditions can enjoy their lives, seek pleasure and beauty, and live the full experience of what it means to be human. The work is serious, but it also can be wildly fun and full of celebration. The merging of the terms *juju* and *bae* is my ode to the ancestral traditions of the old ways while acknowledging the need for newness, youthfulness, and ecstasy—you know, duality.

I believe that ancestors are for everybody, because everybody has ancestors. Honoring, knowing, and accepting this fact that has been solidified through thousands of years of indigenous knowledge can work in tandem with many spiritual faiths. A Christian, a Jewish person, a Bahá'í, a Muslim person, a Hindu, or a Hoodoo can probably all agree that we came from somebody. I believe they would also agree that the choices of those people from whom they have descended deeply impact their life, their locale, what they are interested in, their traumas, and their traditions. I also think that many would agree that the past informs our present and future. Without seeking information about what came before us, how can we know what's ahead? We cannot escape the past, and acknowledging that past is what ancestral veneration is all about. It is why doctors may ask if a particular physical condition runs in the family. It is why people study history. Acknowledgment of life in the past is why we have funerals and other ceremonies that honor the dead. The fact that this acknowledgment has turned into an association with evil demonic entities can only be explained by very intentional warfare that was enacted upon the minds and bodies of Indigenous people to erase that past.

## WOO-WOO WORDS (TERMINOLOGY)

Let's discuss some terms that relate to African spiritual systems that will come up throughout this book.

**Ancestors:** Generally these are deceased family or community members whose presence is still honored within that community. These individuals have the ability to intercede in the affairs of the living.

**ATR (African Traditional Religion):** These are precolonial sub-Saharan religions and cosmological understandings that are rooted in African practice.

**ADR (African Diasporic/Derived Religion):** This designation covers various kinds of spiritual practices that derive from African traditions yet have expanded across the diaspora through Afro-descended people. Also referred to as African Tradition (AT) or African Diasporic Tradition (ADT).

**Animism:** Beliefs that inanimate or otherwise natural objects have a spirit and are alive.

**Africana:** African-derived practices.

As you develop a practice of communing with your ancestors, you'll learn that they may guide you to specific religions, traditions, or ways of life. There are hundreds of practices that believe in the veneration of ancestors, and those may lead you to other religions like Ifa, Vodun, Palo, Candomblé, Akan, Santeria, Hoodoo, Vodou, and Odinala. Although I am a practitioner of Hoodoo and Ifa, I will not focus too deeply on too many ATRs or ADRs in this book. However, understanding the basis of some of these traditions is important, as they specifically inform my worldview and how I present information. Although all these belief systems are ancestor focused and hold many similarities, they are all very unique. I do not intend to jumble every belief system into *one big African religion*, as the continent and the diaspora are vast and *extremely* diverse. The examples provided will instead be used as a reference and guide so that you can commune with *your* ancestral spirit. If, once you feel connected to your ancestors, you are guided down the path of a new specific religion, you will be rooted in the ancestors, which is of extreme importance in all Africana-based practices. As long as you've got them, you're good.

Although I no longer identify as a Christian, fully divorcing myself from Christianity is not only virtually impossible for me but of no interest to me. There are some Christian prayers and Christian juju that have gotten me where I am today. There are prayers to saints and psalms and proverbs that you can bet I'm going to recite or chant when seeking guidance from my spirits. Some of my ancestors were Christian, so I use the Bible and other Christian objects as tools to better connect with my people. You'll soon learn, if you don't already know, that I never throw out the baby with the bathwater—meaning that, if there is helpful information, understanding, or medicine within any situation or religion, I'm absolutely going to take it and make it my own, even if I do not identify with that specific religion personally. If this sounds like you, we can address this in more detail later in the book.

# CHAPTER 2

# MY PRACTICE: IFA AND THE ORISHA

I've already mentioned Ifa a few times in this book. It is one of my religions and has given me grounding and healing and has renewed my ministry within the spiritual arts. Ifa has provided the roadmap that I sought and was the worldview that allowed me to get clear on my destiny and commit to it with my entire being. This tradition outlines how I perceive our journeys through life, which informs some of the contents of this book. This ancient religion, although a generally closed practice to those not fully initiated into it, is helpful to know more about regardless, as it outlines the power of natural forces and the inherent interconnectedness of the universe. Ifa is a widely practiced religion among the diaspora and a good access point to the world of ancestral traditions. There is also an aspect of the religion that musical icon Beyoncé Knowles introduced me to in 2016 via her visual album *Lemonade,* so of course we *have* to talk about it.

## IFA

Ifa's roots extend from coastal West Africa, more specifically of the Yoruba people in Nigeria, Togo, and Benin. As one of (if not the) oldest religions still practiced today, Ifa is rooted in ancestral veneration as well as being in harmonious relationships with nature, yourself, your communities, and intermediary deities called the Orisha. One can achieve this harmony through a concept called *Iwa Pele*, which describes the necessity of having good or gentle character. There's so much to love about Ifa, but one of the tenets of this practice that I constantly remind myself is the belief that "it is your birthright to be joyful, successful, and loved!" This right here completely changed the game for me. I've never heard so explicitly that I am worthy of a good life—just because I was born.

Because, like many indigenous African traditions, Ifa is communicated to its practitioners as part of an oral history, it is hard to know exactly how old the religion is. There is no official "Ifa Bible" that is written down. Simply, Ifa is a divinatory system that contains the mysteries of life as expressed through the sixteen *odu,* or principles that govern our existences. These mysteries are uncovered by a skilled practitioner called a *babalawo* or *iyanifa,* who consults with Ọrunmila (the Orisha of divination) to uncover our individual life paths. And although plenty of practitioners have scribed many of the odu, its full system of beliefs is not written down in the same way as the Christian Bible. And Ifa is wide ranging, with teachings based on ancient mathematics, natural sciences, and an extensive corpus of divine knowledge that informs our lives and the world.

Ifa-Isese is the traditional practice of Ifa as it occurs on the continent. However, because of migration, expansion, and even the transatlantic slave trade, Ifa has moved beyond West Africa and has influenced the world wherever our Yoruba ancestors were moved or displaced. Various iterations of the traditional Isese practice have birthed new religions across the diaspora, from the country of Brazil through Candomblé or the island of Cuba as Lucumí. These traditions are all rooted in the West African practice of Isese but have rightfully created new diasporic understandings of the ancient practice. My current practice is traditional African Isese; however, I was first introduced to the practice through Cuban

Lucumí, as well as African-American iterations of Isese. All these various branches inform how I view the divine corpus of Ifa.

In Ifa, there are some basic understandings often centered on being in harmonious relationship with the natural world, the spirit world, our communities, and ourselves. The acknowledgment and veneration of ancestors as well as Orisha (intermediary deities) are central aspects of being in the right relationship with the world. Through Ifa, humans can receive information about these "mysteries" through Ọrunmila, who is the Orisha of knowledge and wisdom. The way that I like to think of it is that Ifa is like the library of the universe and Ọrunmila is the librarian. In order to get information, we must seek out a diviner, or someone who understands where the books are, and Ọrunmila helps us get exactly what we need and checks the books out for us! Through Ifa, Ọrunmila gives us insight into our lives. This information allows us to actualize better realities for ourselves and live the lives we are destined to live! There are sixteen principles that are used in Ifa divination that can inform the priest how to interpret a message for the client. The following are the laws extracted and interpreted from *The Fundamentals of the Yorùbá Religion: Òrìṣà Worship* by Chief FAMA. These in particular are guiding principles of my spiritual *ile,* or house.

1. Obey Ifa guiding laws to live long in good health
2. Do not say what you do not know
3. Do not perform anything for which you do not have the basic knowledge
4. Do not deceive people
5. Do not claim wisdom that you lack
6. Be humble and do not relish in ego
7. Do not be deceitful and engage in treachery

8. Do not use the sacred feathers of Ifa (Ikoode) for cleaning after using the toilet, so as not to break taboos (or bring harm to oneself)

9. Do not defecate on the Holy Palm or Epo, so as not to break taboos

10. Do not run into a burning house, as life cannot be replaced

11. Have respect for the disabled and less fortunate

12. Have respect for the elder ones in order to not stop blessings from arriving

13. Do not take the partner of an Ogboni member to disrupt the law of Onile

14. Do not take the partner of a friend, for this shall betray the friendship

15. Do not discuss secrets behind the back of others, as it is not your place

16. Have respect for all women, especially the wives of a babalawo

These laws help humans to make sense of a quite confusing world. It is amazing how our ancestors learned and listened for hundreds of years in order to pass down divine wisdom that we can access today. I owe a lot of my growth, healing, and transformation to the power of Ifa and the Orisha.

## ORISHA

An Orisha is an intermediary deity between humans and the divine manifestations of the natural world. Every natural occurrence can be understood through an Orisha deity, as these divine natural occurrences are reflections of Olodumare (God/Creator) manifesting on earth.

Although many ATRs require initiation to learn the secrets, rites, and rituals of each Orisha, everyday people may honor these divine forces of nature through the path of practicing Iwa Pele, or gentle character. There are said to be hundreds of Orisha because they represent so many manifestations of life; however, I will highlight a few of the more popular ones here.

*Èṣù/Elleguá/Eleguá:* The connector between the physical and spirit world, Èṣù is the messenger that takes our sacrifices and prayers to the Creator, Olodumare. He owns the pathway or crossroads of life and can be understood as the manifestation of thresholds between worlds or experiences. He is often referred to as a trickster (sometimes mistakenly reduced to a devil), but he is an honorable spirit who teaches us about free will and choice.

*Ogún:* The Orisha of iron, metals, technology, and war, Ogún is a fierce deity that reigns over concepts of productivity and work. Ogún is found in the forest (in some traditions by railroad tracks) and with his machete is summoned to clear the way to our blessings. Colors representing Ogún are primarily black and green, and sometimes red.

*Obatalá:* This Orisha can be seen as the ultimate parent of every person. Obatalá is the owner of our Ori, white cloth, and all humanity, as he created it. Obatalá is the source of all that is pure, wise, peaceful, and compassionate. Although everyone's parent, Obatalá often aids those who are disabled, and teaches us about the importance of respecting and honoring all kinds of bodies. He has a warrior side, through which he enforces justice in the world. The color white is primarily associated with Obatalá. Depending on the lineage, this Orisha may be referred to as male or female.

*Yemoja/Yemayá:* She is the mother of all, who rules over some rivers, oceans, and seas. Her name translates to "mother whose children are the fish," to acknowledge that she nurtures and cares for all humanity. This water deity represents fertility, motherhood, and protection. She is a very wise Orisha whose capacity to love knows no bounds. Because of her mothering spirit, she is known to fiercely protect her children. Her colors are often represented as white and blue.

*Ọṣun/Oshun/Ochún:* Ọṣun rules over the sweet waters of the world—the brooks, streams, and rivers—embodying love, fertility, money, and beauty. She is the youngest of the female Orishas but retains the title of *iyalode,* or great queen. She heals through her medicinal waters and brings sweetness to the world with honey. She is a masterful healer and fiercely protects her children. She is wise and, without her, we would not know the appreciation of all that is artful, masterful, and beautiful.

*Oyá:* Oyá, who also may be referred to as Yansa or "mother of nine," rules the energy of the winds, lightning, and violent storms. Oyá is traditionally understood as a river deity, a force of change and death. Her number is nine and in traditional Isese is a cunning businesswoman who owns the marketplace. Oyá is also the gatekeeper of the cemetery and presides over the dead, or *egungun.*

*Ṣangó/Jakuta/Changó:* Genealogically, Ṣangó was the third *alafin,* or king, of the Oyo kingdom, before he was deified into an Orisha after his death. He is one of the most popular Orishas, and is known as a very strong warrior and leader. Ṣangó is also a charismatic Orisha who enjoys dancing, drumming, women, and many of life's pleasures. He rules energies of thunder, lightning, and fire across various sects of Orisha veneration. His color is traditionally red, or red and white across the diaspora.

*Ọrunmila:* The name *Ọrunmila* means "heaven knows our salvation." It is said that when humanity was created, Ọrunmila was there to bear witness and thus knows the mysteries of all humanity. Ọrunmila is the physical representation of the Ifa oracle, and therefore serves as a counselor to humans and the interpreter of Olodumare's (the ultimate Creator's) wisdom. He is the deity of knowledge and divination.

## ORI

Each one of us has our own personal Orisha, called Ori. This Orisha is guaranteed to support each of us because, in the Yoruba belief system, we chose it! It is said that at the beginning of our lives, we picked out our destinies. Some of us picked too fast, some of us deeply considered and weighed all our options, and maybe some of us played rock paper scissors. Regardless, our Ori—which means "head"—holds that chosen destiny and guides us on the path to reach it. The tricky part is that sometimes we choose very difficult Ori, and even more often we get out of alignment with our Ori and need to find our way back into balance.

As humans, we carry many paths and many possibilities. Our destinies are malleable, so they may shift and change depending on the natural course of our lives. For example, through divination your Ori may communicate through the diviner that you will be rich and famous! In this case, the diviner may say that your destiny is to be seen and valued for your views and thoughts in a public platform. This may lead to you noticing throughout your life that you have the propensity to attract large crowds and command a room with your energy and overall vibe! This makes sense, as you have a destiny of being rich and famous, but it doesn't necessarily mean that you will reach the point of being known and loved across the world, because life happens. Instead of being a politician or a television personality, your life may lead you to become the leader of a gang. In that case, your propensity for fame and fortune might manifest as being in charge of a gang that is really good at getting money. As a result, you might have more money than you've ever dreamed of because of the financial success of the gang, and you might be well respected among its members. In this way, your destiny has been realized, even if your gang eventually gets busted by the Feds and your riches evaporate in the face of prison charges. Your Ori can manifest in myriad ways depending upon your actions. This is why we must check in with our Oris to be sure that the goodness of our path is accessible.

Another example: the iconic performer and musician Prince must have had a destiny of fame within his Ori, which manifested through his songs, packed concerts, and appearances on television and in movies. But there are other people who have the same destiny and end up only as the face of a briefly viral meme. Our destinies are unique to each person and can shift at any point because of the sporadic nature of life.

A note on destiny, however: Who is more important, a fashion designer or a brain surgeon? Who is more needed, a songwriter or a dentist? What role is most necessary, a lifeguard or a fisherman? Those of us who live in colonized lands know that we may automatically place more value on certain roles than others. However, by understanding the role of destiny in Ifa, we can let go of the notion that there are ways to have an experience that are more valuable than others. Some people are natural-born teachers, some are star athletes from young ages, while others are skilled writers, steel welders, and singers. All these people have different roles that align with their personal destinies. We need skilled teachers, people who are physically strong, and people who can manipulate metals. We need those who can naturally see spirits and those who have powerful dreams that help guide us. Ifa has taught me to value it all and never judge the way that someone else may be living that doesn't align with my Ori, because it is their Ori and not mine. According to Ifa, none of the roles you may play in life matter more or less than the others. They are all a part of our collective holistic destiny.

If your Ori is a little out of whack—maybe things feel fuzzy, good things don't seem to be coming, decisions feel a little bit more complicated than usual, or you are experiencing overwhelming sadness—then you can talk to your personal deity and "get your head on straight." There are many ways to feed one's Ori with sacrifice, prayers, and offerings. However, one of the simplest ways to connect with your Ori to help address some of your personal issues is to greet it and pray to it every single morning. To greet your Ori in the morning, grab the top of your head with both hands, take a deep breath, and say thanks to your Ori for waking you up. You can then say your own prayer to activate your Ori. My prayers every morning often go something like this:

> Ibase Ori, Ibase Ori, Ibase Ori! (Praise Ori, Praise Ori, Praise Ori!)
>
> Ori, I honor you. It is you who are with me through every event of life!
>
> My Ori is a great Ori. My Ori connects me to Olodumare, the Orisha, and my ancestors.
>
> My Ori blesses me consistently, and shows me how good my life can get each day.
>
> My great Ori accepts assistance from others when necessary, my great Ori keeps me away from danger.
>
> My Ori grants me peace and clarity, and does not confuse me.
>
> Ori, please never turn your back on me.
>
> Ori, comfort me in my times of sadness, and celebrate with me during my times of joy.
>
> I embrace my Ori, and my Ori embraces me.
>
> Ase.

Feel free to use this prayer or one of your own words that speaks life into your head, your mind, and to yourself. I promise it feels good, because effectively you are saying thanks and praying to *you*. Sometimes life gets so difficult that we forget that we have medicine and magic in our own bodies. Remember, your Ori—your deity, your god-self—resides in your own head. Activate that power, and trust that your Ori hears you and is already working on it. You can "feed" your Ori cool water, by tracing a line of water from the front of your head to the nape of your neck, to bring "coolness" to your mind when you get overwhelmed (or before!).

---

## AS YOU CONNECT WITH YOUR ORI

HOW DOES IT FEEL TO PRAY TO YOUR ORI?

HAVE YOU NOTICED ANY SHIFTS WITHIN YOURSELF OR YOUR SURROUNDINGS (EVEN IF SEEMINGLY "SMALL")?

REMEMBER TO GET SPECIFIC IN YOUR ORI REQUESTS, AND THANK, VALIDATE, AND AFFIRM YOUR ORI.

---

# CHAPTER 3

# MY PRACTICE: HOODOO

Hoodoo is a practice that is in my heart, because it is what outlines my experience as a Black American raised and nurtured in the United States. Before I studied and understood Hoodoo as a complex Africana healing and harming liberation system, I knew it as the Hoodoo of my family, elders, and ancestors. It nursed me back to health, and taught me the importance of prayer and that some of the most potent magic is always in the "mundane."

Hoodoo is a Black-American spiritual tradition and way of life that descended from enslaved Africans in America. This active creation and understanding of Black Americanism by enslaved Africans creates a particularly charged way of understanding life and Spirit.

I am Black American, so my ancestors carry many belief systems and knowledge from various parts of the world. Although many of my ancestors were survivors of chattel slavery, stolen from West and Central Africa, they were dropped primarily in the United States, while others were dropped in the Caribbean. Those enslaved African ancestors were often medicine people who knew about plant medicines, healing herbs, rituals, protective talismans, and other spiritual traditions that were native to their countries. Based on my Ancestry.com test, I have quite a bit of Nigerian and Congolese ancestry and thus can assume that medicines from regions in Nigeria and the Congo informed the kind of rituals that my ancestors partook in in their homelands as well as in the United States. Many African-American people are a combination of various cultural norms, spiritual belief systems, and even different deities because of the tribal mixing that happened as a result of colonialism and forced migration. The ancestors became a part of one "Black" race in the United States, whereas formerly people were identified based on tribe, region, and lineage affiliations. Blackness formed not only as a result of colonialism, but as a survival mechanism on this new soil. Camaraderie and connections were built, new languages were learned, and tribal separations mattered less and less as the Black race formed as a new identifying unit to combat slavery, Jim Crow, and other traumatic systems that we still see today. That unification, medicine-making, freedom-building, and fight for survival can be described as Hoodoo.

Many of my Hoodoo ancestors believe that we have the ability and right to protect what is ours, be free, and also enjoy our lives on our own terms by any means necessary. This energetic way to live removes feelings of guilt, shame, or doubt from my mind when I'm experiencing the positive aspects of life. It has helped me address my "survivor's guilt," which is a guilt that often seeps into the lives of those who survived any form of tragedy or traumatic experience. My ancestors showed me that I have a right to survive, and I should not be ashamed for surviving, for living, for experiencing joy, or for finding pleasure. I will not only fight for my joy but for that joy and pleasure to be accessible to more people, because we all deserve those if we are acting right and doing our best. Hoodoo gives me not only the permission to fight against personal and collective enslavements, but acknowledges that warfare has been a necessary component of that fight. It acknowledges the fact that anti-Blackness and indigeneity is real, and that there are traditions that acknowledge that truth through protective rituals and practices. These practices, all with ancestors at their center, encourage me to abandon all that does not serve me, because something better is always near if I make the right choices and keep Spirit close. So regardless of what issues I may face, I can lean on the belief systems of my religions as a backbone to support me in having a good and pleasurable life, which is a big deal from a Catholic-raised child—raised on tenets of constant repentance and shame.

If you can't tell, in the world of Africana spiritual systems it is absolutely possible to acknowledge and be a member of multiple faith traditions as long as they serve you well. Especially as a Black person, I have intentionally not relegated myself to any specific spiritual tribal connection because I acknowledge the equal parts of me. This is a personal decision that may differ when you speak to other practitioners. It is very easy to get into the "my African religion is better" conversation, but I think you have to do what works for you and your destiny.

Hoodoo is not quite the same thing as Voodoo, although there are quite a few similarities. You may hear people use the terms interchangeably, and it may be hard to initially understand the distinction. As I explained earlier, both Hoodoo and Voodoo contain rituals, heavily African influenced, and can contain beliefs and practices from Christianity. Voodoo specifically deals with a religion that is influenced by West African Vodun (a religion in its own right) that also translated into Haitian Vodou (again, an independent religion), that then intermixed with folks in Louisiana through French Catholicism, which birthed the tradition of Voodoo. Voodoo is like the American baby of Vodou, although some people refer to Vodou or Vodun as Voodoo, too. Context greatly matters. Regardless, Hoodoo and Voodoo are examples of how our ancestral traditions never died but instead morphed to remain relevant to African-descended people in America.

As I must reiterate—as any good Hoodoo lady would—Hoodoo is not inherently bad or evil. Hoodoo is whatever you make it, and can be used to amplify whatever intentions you may already have. If your intention is to harm, then Hoodoo can help you harm; if your intentions are to heal, then Hoodoo will amplify your healing. The objective in how you practice Hoodoo lies in your intention and what your ancestors and the spirits sanction you to do, but Hoodoo is essentially about power. What you do with that power is on you, and the repercussions of using that power are on you, too. I'm not in the business of telling anyone how they should use Hoodoo, as I've seen it work miracles on both ends of the spectrum. I've also witnessed and historically know the healing and freedom that the power of Hoodoo and the spirits behind it have yielded for others. This is especially apparent in the stories of High John the Conqueror.

High John is a spirit with many faces and facets. He can be seen as a collective ancestor, with a deep collection of lore concerning his life and the powers he carries to support those he wants to protect. There is one story about High John that names him as a former slave. However, he was a slave that was always perceived as smarter than his master. High John would play tricks on him, set him up, and confuse him, which would not only piss off his master but also give a lot of pride to the other enslaved folks who knew that John could get out of anything. There are also stories that High John was the former Congolese king enslaved in America but who never lost his kingly wit and power. There's also lore of John marrying the devil's daughter and running away with her, narrowly escaping the clutches of Lucifer himself. This trickster and resilient energy that our ancestor John embodies can be summoned with the very popular Hoodoo plant known as the High John the Conqueror root. Those in possession of this root can summon the powers of High John and defeat any enemy. High John told the slaves that, although he was leaving the plantation, they could call on him anytime and he would come to those who were being abused by their masters or were enduring other forms of hardships through severe injustice. This root has been used by many in order to achieve victory in their endeavors and fight back against abuse. Frederick Douglass was even said to have been in possession of this root when he successfully fought back against his slave master. These stories about High John, whether the original or people who embodied High John–like energy, contribute to how we view the collective ancestor of High John, whose energy and power is summoned by many of us who know his name and have been granted access. Many collective ancestors like High John, John Henry, Caroline Dye, Zora Neale Hurston, and Cathay Williams can all be considered important icons within the Hoodoo pantheon who are also collective ancestors to us.

However, not every Black person identifies as a Hoodoo conjurer, as a conjurer is someone who specifically uses the spirits of the divine and natural elements to control or manipulate a behavior. Ancestors knew a lot about plant medicine because they were equipped to work with the land. So they knew the berries and plants that could be used to poison livestock and slave masters! Conjurers were often sought as medicine people to stop a partner from cheating or to give spiritual advice on winning the lottery or making business deals. Conjurers were and are sought to keep bad people out of your house or to find love. I descended from a root lady who went by the name of MerLiza and was from Mathews County, Virginia, in the mid-1800s. Because Black folks didn't often have access to white doctors, my great-grandmother would work out of her home to provide herbal remedies to families and to birth babies. She was so successful and highly regarded that white doctors would often send patients to my great-grandmother's house when they couldn't figure out themselves what was wrong.

Healing, protection, fighting, liberation, cleansing, dancing, eating, singing, prophesying, baby birthing, and the like are all aspects of Hoodoo. It is no surprise that popular Black dance moves today have their roots in the rituals of traditional African tribes from regions that we may have descended from. The belief that it's bad luck to sweep a person's foot with a broom, that it's good luck to eat black-eyed peas on

New Year's Day, and that spilling salt can bring bad fortune all have a root in a traditional belief system. Many of these "superstitions" are simply rituals that have been around for many years as a means of protection and securing blessings. This is important because Hoodoo holds a very rich history, and thus we can understand much about our past through ancestral archiving and resilience. Hoodoo is not "one size fits all," nor does every ritual work for everybody. This is also true for many African-centered traditions, as we are not a monolith, and neither are our belief systems or rituals. Hoodoo specifically is quite regional, meaning that certain practices that make sense in South Carolina may be unfamiliar in Virginia. There are rituals found in Mississippi Hoodoo culture that seem to exist in that state alone. For example, shoe tracking (the process of gaining someone's essence through collecting their shoe footprints in the dirt) may not be practiced in a region where people are less likely to wear shoes because of sweltering hot weather. Another example is the ritual of the "nature sack." Nature sacks were very common in the Mississippi Delta region, where often a woman would wear a small sack around her waist filled with the personal items of her lover (nail clippings, cuttings of clothes, herbs, and even bodily fluids). A nature sack was said to keep your lover faithful, so many Mississippi women believed that they could control their lover's "nature" with this small sack tied around their waist. Although we can debate about issues of consent and the reasoning behind engaging in spiritual work such as this, the point here is that this particular ritual is regional, and it has only later been adopted in other regions due to the spread of information through music and the media.

The intermixing of the Black Church and Hoodoo still exists today, as the line between conjurer and preacher was blurred in slave times. Not until emancipation did we start to see a more clear delineation between those who were "people of God" and those who practiced "that old-time stuff." Many Hoodoos will tell you that Hoodoo and Christianity go hand in hand, and that Hoodoo *must* include Christianity in order to properly be regarded as Hoodoo. This is simply not the case. Hoodoo heavily impacted Christianity, and I'd even argue that Hoodoo impacted Christianity more than Christianity impacted Hoodoo, at least initially. But Hoodoo is a valid tradition on its own without use of the Bible or other Christian objects. Islam also influenced Hoodoo, as well as people who never converted to Christianity and instead held on to their African beliefs, or at the very least used Christianity more as a way to make sense of their new reality than an abandonment of their African traditional methods and modalities. The founder of the largest Pentecostal church in the United States, the Church of God in Christ (COGIC), Charles Harrison Mason, was in fact a man who practiced Conjure, a branch of Hoodoo. In fact, Charles Harrison Mason created the COGIC as a way to honor his ancestors' ways of worshiping through prayer rituals, song, dance, spontaneous shouting, prophesying, and emotive expression—all of which was very African. It is also said that he would use "natural objects" to discern God's will, and heal using roots and other natural modalities. Hoodoo and Black Christianity have become intertwined through escape routes hidden in spirituals, water baptismal rituals, and prophesying; this does not mean that Hoodoo needs Christianity in order to function.

Regardless of what is shown in the public eye, there are many accounts of church folks, regula' folks, and even the preachers seeking the medicine of the root lady or the "two-headed doctor" to handle the issues that God seemed to keep His hands off. Many psychics, witches, and conjurers today will tell you that our client list is long, and it isn't just the people with headwraps and crystal necklaces—it's everybody, especially those you would least expect. This has always been the case, and I'm sure always will be. People know where to go to get things done.

# CHAPTER 4

# HOW I MET MY ANCESTORS

I met my ancestors for the first time in 2017. Now, of course they have always been around, but this is when I really listened. In 2013, I built my first ancestral altar in my dorm room at Spelman College, but I didn't really know what I was doing or fully understand why I was doing it. I read about altars in an Iyanla Vanzant book and decided that I needed one, too. That whole thing eventually fell off after a year or so.

I was not a child who talked to the dead or saw spirits, like many folks deep into the juju work seem to have been. The only spirits I talked to during that period of my life were saints, whom Catholics saw more as elevated beings whom we could pray to instead of worrying God. I prayed to Jesus's mama, Mary, of course, and some of the saints whom I needed to help me, but I didn't see them, and they didn't talk back to me. The only reason that I knew or "felt" that they were real was because my prayers were always answered. Otherwise I had no particular interest in the "dead" as a child. I was too busy being in a child's place and delving into the world of girls, boys, and my ever-present sadness and disdain for life.

So, I met my ancestors when I was grown. I was still deeply unhappy, as many graduate students are, especially Black ones at predominantly white institutions. During this time, I was at the beginning of dedicating five years of my life to a doctoral degree in clinical psychology. I had just moved to Chicago, Illinois, and was prepared to embark on the kind of healing journey that traditional Western medicine allowed me to partake in. I was very familiar with mental health struggles—I was diagnosed with major depressive disorder, post-traumatic stress disorder, and generalized anxiety as a child. And while I have struggled with my own mental health for most of my life, I knew that there were resources, people, and medicines that could support me. That access, as well as the knowledge that it existed, played a huge role in my ability to find care as a youth, so I wanted to provide it to other people, especially children who were struggling. I wanted to encourage Black families, in particular, to seek education and knowledge about the complexities of our brains and our traumas. I wanted to share the resources and tools that I didn't always have through therapeutic technologies. And I believed that this was my ultimate calling as a healer. So, after I graduated undergrad from Spelman College with my bachelor's degree in psychology, it was no question that higher education would be my reality for several more years.

However, while attending graduate school, a slew of my own mental health issues arose as I dealt with academic racism, ridiculous professors, money issues, family traumas exacerbated by my studies, and a failing romantic relationship. Mental health did not exist for me at that time. I was simply going through the motions: practicing with mock clients, analyzing data that I could barely comprehend. I found it hard to communicate with people, which is usually easy for me. I didn't feel safe, I couldn't focus, I couldn't think. I was severely unhappy, and this unhappiness deeply affected my schoolwork, my connections to other people, and my overall quality of life. I was struggling.

One night in 2017, I finished my work as I normally did. I probably had a few too many glasses of wine while studying, as I normally did. And I went to sleep, preparing to wake up early in the morning, as I did almost every day. But things shifted for me after this particular night. Until this experience, I had never been much of a dreamer. Sure, I had the usual dreams that didn't make sense, mostly consisting of disjointed visuals that I hardly remembered. I absolutely was not someone who had prophetic dreams or who saw visions or interacted with spirits in my waking life. I was not connected much at all to the ancestral realms—that is, until I met them on this lonely night.

In this dream, I saw the face of my maternal grandmother on the left and the face of my paternal grandmother on the right. I was looking at only their faces, both from the neck up, emerging from a pitch-black background. I looked at them with intensity and love. They were still, stoic. It almost felt like the portion of a video game where you choose your fighter. Their faces didn't have much expression, but they were present. Before I was about to choose my "grandmother fighter," the face of my maternal grandmother, Grandma Ruth, disappeared, leaving me and my grandmommy, Ellestine. Her face was still unmoving. I looked at her for some time until it felt like something snatched me into her eyes. It was almost as if I were going inside her mind and inside her personal history as I traveled into more darkness through the portal of her eyes. And then I arrived.

Suddenly I was actively witnessing life on a plantation. I could not be seen, as I watched most of this story from an aerial view. I somehow knew that this plantation was in South Carolina. I don't know how I knew, but I was certain that this information was completely factual, as this is where a lot of my family on my paternal side is from. From my perspective far above the land, I watched enslaved people being actively brutalized, yelled at, and whipped. I saw people walking through the fields, picking and carrying bundles of cotton. There were Black children running in the fields, too. I was very clearly and obviously witnessing slavery.

Then I was inside what looked like a small slave cabin: very dark floors and walls, most likely made of wood and maybe some pieces of brick. After taking in the makings of a small slave cabin, I noticed two middle-aged white men and a Black woman who looked like me. Her hair was thick and pushed up and back. She was dark skinned with a thin frame, and short . . . like my grandmother. There was a bed, a chair, and perhaps a small table, too . . . but what really stood out to me was the white linen. It was such crisp white linen that lined this uncomfortable-looking bed, and there was more white linen on the small chair, perhaps in preparation to be folded or put on the bed itself. I don't know why this stark white image stood out so much to me, but the minute I stopped noticing the white linen was the minute I watched two men brutally gang-rape this unnamed woman whom I (in the dream) understood to be one of my foremothers on my daddy's side.

She was quiet the entire time that they brutalized her and beat her. She never yelled or even whimpered. The room was in complete disarray when they finished. And so they beat her again because of the mess that was made. Once they fixed their pants, they left, ordering her to not be so filthy next time. She remained quiet. After they left, she just started pulling the sheets off the bed and gathering them to wash. She scrubbed her blood and reassembled the place, bringing it back to normal. I continued to watch all this from my aerial view.

Within the dream, it seemed like some days or maybe weeks had passed, but I learned that this unnamed ancestral mother of mine died of what seemed like a broken heart. She died because she was unfathomably sad. She left behind two or three children. I don't know how I learned this in the dream—I just knew that's what happened. Once I got this piece of information, I immediately woke up in the morning with tears in my eyes and an uncontrollable feeling of sadness. What the hell did I just witness?

As you can see, this dream or vision still hasn't left me many years later.

I had class that morning, and interestingly enough, it was with my only African-American professor in graduate school. Dr. Moore's class was the one I liked best. She always brought the importance of racial understanding within psychological work to the forefront, and she had a way of really empowering and uplifting her Black students in the class.

She was my absolute favorite, and I think I might have been hers, too. I was usually very talkative in her courses, but that day was different. There was no hand raising or pontificating coming from me. My sadness and the visions of my foremother lingered. Dr. Moore told me to stay after class. Of course, I started crying again as soon as I began to recount my night and my morning to her. She listened intently, actively, without interrupting, and then looked at me straight-faced and said, "Your ancestors are talking to you."

At this point I was familiar with the concept of ancestors, but I never felt they had talked to me directly, at least not like this. Dr. Moore continued to talk intentionally and slowly to me. "You are in a program to learn how to validate and affirm the feelings and the traumas of everybody around you, including strangers, yet you have not validated your own people, your family, or yourself," she explained. At that moment, I completely understood everything. We gathered our things and she immediately took me to the school librarian, Ms. Kerry, a kind woman with a very soft and welcoming demeanor, to whom I recounted my dream at Dr. Moore's request. I learned that Ms. Kerry was a genealogist and could help me learn more about my family history, so that I could get more information about the woman in my dream.

We started meeting weekly to build my family tree, sharing names and stories about what Ms. Kerry had been able to find through public records. My tree began to sprout the names of my family that I never knew, names that triggered the memories of my grandmothers and inspired stories that may not have been told otherwise. I still use Ms. Kerry's resource as a way to tie up loose ends within my own lineage, and then use spiritual means to investigate these ancestors further. She was able to generate a family history that had been largely confused or simply unknown for decades. All this happened because of a brutal dream about my ancestral mother, a Black woman who suffered during slavery . . . and the kindness of two Black women dedicated to connecting me to the dead. This is what spearheaded my ancestral journey, and I've never turned back (although I have looked back pretty intensely). I have since dedicated so much of my life to retrieve what was lost, so that it can never be lost again.

I share this story because it still blows my mind to think about today, but most importantly it highlights the very intense and dramatic ways that my ancestors called me. Sure, they tried to reach me in 2013, but I'm learning that sometimes as humans we need the dramatics in order to pay attention. My ancestors made sure to show me something so striking that it could get the message across clearly. After I had that dream, I knew it was them calling. As you've read, it was not a sweet calling or one that made me feel uplifted or inspired. It was tumultuous, real, traumatic, and sad. They did not whisper sweet nothings in my ear, or sing me lullabies on a sandy shore and call me "sweet baby." Instead, they showed me all the emotional shit they've been carrying, that my grandmother's been carry-ing, and subsequently what I've been carrying since birth. They showed me that the deep sadness that I've felt since childhood was not always my own. It gave structure to the actions of my family throughout genera-tions. It was up to me, though, to do something with that information, and, as Dr. Moore put it, to "validate" the experiences of my family and our complete stories—good, bad, and ugliest.

The stories within our lineage are immense. It's hard to even fathom what some of the experiences may have been, especially for those who descend from people who were constantly fighting to survive throughout their entire lives. These survival strategies are passed down through our bloodlines. Societies, communities, and families can be in constant states of reliving the past and not even be aware of the cycles they are living out. But what my ancestors taught me is that if we don't seek to understand what has come before, we may unintentionally carry out parts of the past that we actually need to let go. It *is* possible to validate and heal through the events that have already happened, and to learn from those experiences in order to live more comprehensive and exciting lives.

Ancestral veneration has been a pivotal part of me growing into the best version of myself. Although I've experienced many different religions throughout my life, it was not until I intentionally connected with my ancestors that I felt more confident, loved, and supported. Honoring my ancestors is assisting me in honoring myself, which has been an impossible task for most of my life. Ancestral veneration is the link to what we believe has been lost.

## CHAPTER 5

# WHAT IS ANCESTOR VENERATION?

To put it simply, ancestor veneration is the process of giving reverence to the deceased who still have the ability to influence and intervene in the affairs of the living. Veneration, however, is not worship! As Olúwo jogbodo Ọrunmila, an elder in the Yoruba tradition, states, "In Yoruba culture we pay homage to the people before us; we don't worship them. As a matter of fact, worshiping in the Abrahamic context is very alien to Yoruba culture." This is critical to understand, because the word *worship* is often used to describe the actions of those who practice ancestral spiritualisms when they are honoring ancestors.

Worship often has a connotation of fully submitting to something as a "god-like" figure. Please understand when I say that the ancestors are not gods! The ancestors are also not God. The ancestors did not necessarily create the moon and the sea. The ancestors are our ancestors, and they deserve a rightful and honorable position in our lives. I love the concept of ancestral veneration because it allows us to find the power and honor with spirits that are not God. If we were socialized through Western religion, we often only trust God, talk to God, and feel that only this outside all-powerful male entity can understand us. Conversely, when venerating ancestors, we can connect with multiple spirits that love and support us. We can find protection not only outside ourselves but within our own bodies, the trees outside our homes, the flowers we pass on the way to work, and the beach that we visit on vacation—because our ancestors live in the natural world. Ancestral veneration also gives me the ability to have more compassion for humanity, as our ancestors were once human and still manage to sacrifice for us even through their own personal trials and issues. The godliness that we seek is not only found in a God, but in our everyday lives, situations, and the people around us. This, to me, creates a more holistic understanding of the spirit world and how its holiness penetrates every aspect of our lives. Let us continue to find space to venerate more than one powerful, all-knowing God, and also honor the spirits that live in us, too. That, in itself, has helped me understand God much more deeply.

Ancestors are entities and spirits who advocate for and support us even after their death, and because of that we honor their work and the sacrifices they have made in the course of taking care of us. The acceptance of the ancestors as well as other cultural deities within traditional African practices is often incorrectly classified as polytheistic (belief in multiple gods). Although there are of course some polytheistic ATRs, I believe that the lack of understanding and projection of westernized Abrahamic religious thought patterns has determined all African and descended religions as polytheistic, when that is simply not true. On the contrary, African and African-descended spiritual beliefs such as Ifa, Odinani, Vodun, Akan, Candomblé, Palo Mayombe, Hoodoo, and Santeria are monotheistic (or at least henotheistic, meaning they believe in one Source but accept the existence of other deities) but are often incorrectly mislabeled as polytheistic practices. Monotheism and henotheism are acknowledgments that there is a belief in a powerful Creator/Source/God while addressing the very important roles of other forces and entities that are still valued and worthy of veneration and acknowledgment. This acknowledgment of other spirits, however, does not denounce the fact that there is still *only one primary Creator source*. Western understandings of these diasporic systems have created incorrect assumptions about the roles of ancestors and other deities in our lives, which further confuses these practices as idol worship and a lack of godliness.

For example, within Haitian Vodou, Bondye is the name for the all-powerful being who created the universe and everything in it. Because Bondye is so powerful and transcendent, he has no direct connection with humans who may need assistance with their issues and problems. This is why the *loas*, or spirits within Haitian Vodou, serve as intermediaries between humans and Bondye. When watching or participating in a Vodou ceremony, one may see veneration and celebration of a specific (or sometimes multiple) loa. Someone who does not understand this may think Vodou practitioners are polytheistic, because it could look like they are praising multiple gods. However, these ceremonial endeavors are not to be understood as worship of different gods, but rather acknowledgment of God's power as it works through these spiritual intermediaries who interact with us in our daily experiences here on earth.

This dynamic is similar to how we should view our ancestors. I've learned that the English language, coupled with dominant Abrahamic belief systems, makes it extremely difficult to accurately communicate how other folks throughout the world create cosmological understandings. The limitations have caused a breach in the ancient wisdoms that so many of us are journeying to remember, with our ancestors at the head of the class.

Venerating ancestral spirits dates back to the mid-4000s BCE in ancient Mesopotamia, one of the oldest documented civilizations in the entire world. So this ain't new shit. See, the beautiful part about venerating ancestors is that this belief has extended beyond regions, countries, centuries, religions, and languages. Most cultures have some form of honoring their deceased loved ones and acknowledge the presence of those loved ones even after they have departed. There are hundreds of thousands of cultures spanning from ancient China to ancient Greece that have very extensive rituals to honor the dead. Acknowledging the role of the deceased is a belief that most cultures can generally agree on regardless of religion, creed, race, or native tongue. It is one of the oldest systems that we have.

Although I am writing this book as a practitioner of multiple African and diasporic practices focused on people descended from Africans, I encourage all individuals to research their indigenous pre-Christian/Islamic histories, ancient stories, and cosmologies as a way to connect to ancestral rites and belief systems in ways that honor your specific lineage. Regardless of who you are, you have some ancestors that existed pre- and post-colonialism, and whichever side(s) you may be on when it comes to that colonialism, you've got some ancestors who are probably starved for your attention and can give you a bit more context about who you are outside your individual racial makeup. In this book, I will provide many examples of how ancestral veneration shows up for African-descended people.

None of what I'm sharing is a complete secret, and much of what you can learn about your lineage can be sourced through research and conversation. As you take in this information, I encourage you to trust your "ancestral eye" to evaluate it. This term was inspired by a post from a fellow practitioner, Chelsea Neason, some years ago. Chelsea mentioned that taking in information with discernment and intuition has been extremely helpful to her. In short, taking in information with the ancestral eye is the way to see beyond what's in front of you. Whether with words, ideas, writings, or something else, sometimes your ancestors fill in gaps for you. A secret, spell, or information that is presented to you in a very general way may be difficult to parse, but your mind's eye can spell it out clearly for you even when the words don't, if you can learn to access your ancestral eye. Think of this ability as "that look" that you may receive from a family member or a friend when something sounds like some bullshit, or the one an adult may have given you when you were acting up in public as a child. It's the one you may have on your face if you're really impressed by something or someone. That "look" tells you a million words without even one breath taken.

Use that same energy as you read this book, and as you're processing *any* resource that seeks to share information with you about your ancestral rites or knowledge. If someone is sharing a prayer, does it resonate with you? Do you need to change some of the words around before you chant it? Who does this information come from and what is this person's motive in sharing it with you? Are you having visions or thoughts that feel like you are reading something that you're *supposed to*? Are your ancestors giving you *that look* as you take in the information? Perhaps you feel jittery or you get hot while learning history about your people. Whatever those feelings are, trust them and continue to do your research, leaning on your ancestral eye to guide you. Do not take my or anyone's words alone while on this journey: ask yourself what your ancestral eye says. That ancestral eye is your intuition, and it's a powerful gift that has kept our people safe and connected for hundreds of years—so trust it.

As you'll learn on this journey, there are a lot of rituals, rites, and secrets within ATRs and ADRs. I won't be sharing any of those, but I do want to put you on the path of finding out for yourself. Regardless of who you are or your current religious affiliation, ancestral veneration is for you. And it is especially for those I'm talking to directly: Black folks, Negroes, melanated, the Original People, African-American, Black-skinned—whatever you may call yourself, I mean *you*.

## CHAPTER 6

# WHY DOES ANCESTRAL VENERATION MATTER?

If I can channel my inner Hotep for one second, I'd love to briefly get this out of the way. Why do you think that society has hidden your ancestral traditions from you? Why do you think that greater society has erased thousands of years of indigenous ancestral wisdom? Why do you think oral tradition and history have been seen as less "valid" forms of information sharing? Why, when you think of "science," do you see white men in lab coats and not melanated people using binary coding and the mathematics of probability through throwing shells or coins? Who told your auntie that you're practicing witchcraft because you saw a psychic or even stopped going to church? Whom does this viewpoint benefit, and is it you? You have to see where I'm going with this . . .

As we will discuss later in this book, colonialism has done a number on Black folks, and subsequently all of us. The demonization of Black ancestral practices was deliberate and ongoing. Spirit communication, ancestral veneration, divination, and sacrifice had to be degraded in order to successfully control and subjugate a group of people. People who are sure about who they are, who are spiritually and emotionally well resourced, are not good candidates for enslavement and colonialism. Stripping people from what connected them to their source and each other was a necessary move in the intricate strategy of imperialism. And it worked—very well. The value of your ancestors was degraded while other folks' ancestors, who were not yours, were prioritized.

Have you ever spent a dollar before? Of course you have. And if you look at most forms of currency (not just in the United States), there is often an image of somebody dead on that money. George Washington's face graces the one-dollar bill, Abraham Lincoln is on the penny, Andrew Jackson is on the twenty-dollar bill. This form of memorializing all these dead white men is America's way of venerating America's ancestors. These men are actively being exalted by having their faces and names all throughout United States currency, which are among the most coveted items in the world. Now, I'm not related to them—in fact I hardly think about whose face is on the bill I have to spend—but this is one of the ways in which ancestral veneration is pervasive in our society. And not only that: it sends a clear message about the kinds of ancestors that are worthy of being venerated.

Dead white men on money means something to the collective consciousness. The energies of these particular people are being exalted to the highest degree. Yet these folks have very complicated, even horrific, histories that I don't really want to actively uplift. Some of these folks are known slave owners, yet we have all consented to engaging in the gift of exchange with these white men that have been deemed some of the most important ancestors of America. I often think about the number of dead folks whose names ring bells because they have been deemed important enough to learn about in educational systems, and throughout our cultural history. Their energies and spirits get to experience the process of elevation, a coveted desire of many spirits. So I often wonder how different our society would be if we venerated our *own* spirits with the same fervor and dedication as the people like George Washington or Thomas Jefferson.

Ancestral veneration is not completely new to you. Even if you've never used this kind of term, you've acknowledged and regarded someone who has died. You've also participated in ancestral veneration through learning about someone's legacy, witnessing someone be inducted into a hall of fame, or running in a marathon named after one of the kindest nuns in your school (I've participated in this very specific example). Ancestral veneration is everywhere, which means that ancestors are everywhere. It really doesn't take a psychic to rely on the importance of ancestors as a society. On a basic level, so much of our surface-level daily thoughts and routines are because of the acts of some dead folks. Even the laws to which we are bound as communities are often reflections of a tradition of a specific community that has been enacted by a bunch of dead people.

Traditions are valuable, yet the amount of veneration to spirits who may not have had my identity or yours in mind creates an imbalance. I'd like to see more spirits who looked like me, talked like me, and who were groundbreaking in their respective spaces honored and valued consistently like other folks. I truly think this would provide an energetic shift that could bring some intentional harmony to the world. It is clear through all these examples that we know ancestors are important and that their legacy impacts our lives. But now what will we do with that information? Whom will we choose to venerate?

## AS YOU BEGIN CONNECTING WITH ANCESTORS

WHAT ANCESTOR(S) WOULD YOU LIKE TO KNOW MORE ABOUT? OR WHICH ANCESTOR DO YOU THINK DESERVES MORE SHINE AND VENERATION?

WHY DID YOU CHOOSE THEM?

HOW MAY YOU GO ABOUT LEARNING MORE ABOUT THEM AND SHARING THEIR STORIES?

HOW DO YOU THINK THE POWER OF THEIR STORIES WOULD BE BENEFICIAL TO THE COLLECTIVE?

## ANCESTOR WORK AS EVERYDAY MEDICINE

Intense spiritual deprivation from acknowledging our own ancestors affects not only our spirits but our entire physical bodies and emotions. It affects the kind of society that we live in and the kind of people that we are around. Spiritual deprivation creates communities that are sick, deprived, and unable to experience the goodness of life. Spirit is not separate from the mundane, nature, our food sources, our love lives, our family relationships, and our jobs. The spirit is the battery in the backs of the living. The soul or spirit gives us life; it fuels our journey and improves the quality of our experiences in our flesh. Yet it also seems to be the part of us that easily gets neglected. When we physically die, our spirit lives on, as it was there in the beginning and will be in the end. We all have an innate spirit, and we also have spirits that exist within and around us that guide our life journeys. These spirits can go by many names, but I will primarily be referring to the spirit of the ancestors.

We have so many ways to seek "support" in our lives, but outside church services and a few temples, it can be hard to receive access to holistic care that tends to our spirit. An easy example of this is the extreme focus on our physical fitness and physical health in our society. There are hundreds of medical institutions whose purpose is to help us heal and recover our corporeal well-being. We are regularly encouraged to have regular checkups on our eyes, teeth, and rest of our bodies. There are hundreds of thousands of medicines that exist to help our physical forms reach their optimal level. This hyperfocus can of course be explained through corporate greed and capitalism making access to bodily care a profitable industry, but there is also a serious neglect of spirit care. Doctors' visits, commercials about every medication under the sun, workouts, gyms, and more bombard our consciousness as a society. However, mental health is rising in the realms of health that we now prioritize.

I'm noticing commercials about therapy and mental health that didn't exist ten years ago, so there is an acknowledgment of mental wellness. but there is still hardly any acknowledgment of the spirit, which is at the core of all this.

As you delve more into ancestral systems, you'll see very clearly the connection between the physical, mental, emotional, and the spiritual. In fact, there are some ways to heal ourselves that are rooted in a spiritual issue rather than a problem with our physical or emotional bodies. Sometimes we have physical pains because of certain spirits within our lineage. Sometimes our depression is linked to a group of ancestors who are upset or sad themselves, which in turn affects our mental wellness. Having an ancestrally grounded practice allows us to better pinpoint the reasonings behind our experience, and then, *if it is solely spiritual*, to seek spiritual medicine that can be prescribed from a trusted practitioner.

My point is not to suggest that we don't need doctors or therapists. We need them—and more of them! Rather my point is to suggest that spiritual medicine is an important addition to our medicinal arsenal. It can help gauge the severity of our concerns and point us in the right direction to the proper person who can assist us. Sometimes that's a medical doctor, sometimes that's the two-headed doctor, and most times it's a little bit of both. We may be experiencing headaches because a spirit is trying to get our attention. Sometimes a stomachache is the result of eating certain foods that are taboo to us.

A taboo is a behavior that one should avoid engaging in, per your spirit's choice, in order to support living a better life. For example, after a reading, I was informed that for sixteen days I was not allowed to use curse words, as it would subsequently "curse me." Curse words for those sixteen days were a spiritual taboo, and cursing could have harmed me in some way during those days. It's not that I could never say the word *bitch* again in my life; it's just that I couldn't during those specific days. Say I called someone a bitch during one of the prohibited days while I was behind the wheel, and another driver heard it and sought to harm me physically. That interaction could have been avoided if I did not curse them out. This is why taboos exist, and we learn about these taboos through spiritual teachers and practitioners who consult our spirits to give us insight into our lives. Not adhering to taboos is another way that can explain why we may be having an unfavorable experience.

I remember being a part of a spiritual house and going through an initiation ceremony with someone who was expected to die from cancer in six months. Our babalawo (high priest spiritual advisor within Ifa tradition) advised that my mate was to proceed through various initiation ceremonies, at the request of this person's ancestors, in order to address the spreading of the cancer. He followed through on his spiritual prescriptions and was cancer free a few months after his ceremonies. The steady decline that his body was experiencing was speedily avoided. This example suggests that, yes, he did need competent doctors to care for him through his diagnoses, but spiritual medicine in addition to his medical care is what we believe kept him alive and cancer free. One form of care is not greater than the other; however, spirit medicine does have the ability to give us insights into what may be causing us distress or concern. Sometimes the Spirit will clearly tell us, "Go get that checked out" or "Stop neglecting to take your medicine!"

This reminds me of another story from one of my clients about three years ago. This client was so stressed because they lived with a terrible roommate. They were trying to come up with the money to move out and were concerned about finding an apartment at that particular time of year without having planned for a move. They sought a reading with me so that they could check in with their ancestors about how to get out of this living situation as soon as possible, find additional funds to move, and receive advice on where to live next. As I was consulting the ancestors, I heard very clearly that my client was not to worry about it. The spirits instructed that my client calm down and stop worrying about trying to move out, because they wouldn't be moving and that the roommate situation was being taken care of. My client trusted this advice. One week later, they alerted me that their roommate randomly decided to move to Mexico and would be moving out within the next two weeks. Imagine the amount of stress my client averted by not attempting to move when they didn't need to. This is how ancestral advice has the power to support us and lessen some of our worries.

The power of ancestral medicine and the ability to heal is one of the most powerful tools that we have. It gives us clear insight and can lessen so many concerns. Let me be clear, though: this is not *magic*. I mean, it could be classified as such, but simply because you have ancestral medicine does not mean that your life is automatically perfect. Spiritual medicine does not allow you to live life completely free of stress. In fact, the medicine will remind you that, as a human, stress and worry is kind of what we signed up for when we came to this plane. What it does do, though, is give us resources to address those worries and that stress. Spiritual medicine through ancestral connection takes time. It is quite literally a lifelong journey and perhaps exists into the afterlife. Do not think that because you prayed to your ancestors one day, life will be perfect the next day. Many successful practitioners have been at this work for a few years and thus have a handle on their ancestral court and spirit team. One month or even a year does not guarantee immediate success. As you *will* learn throughout your journey, your ancestors make shit a lot more favorable for you, and less impossible. They'll give you doses of reality, a lot of love, and, of course, miracles.

I'm not sure about your life, but my life ain't been no crystal stair. And although I had praying grandmothers and a loving family who did their best, it would have been nice to know that I could call on a great-grandmother and complain about how her descendants are getting on my nerves, then ask if she can step in and help. It would have also been nice to know that there was a place for me to feel less alone, through knowing who my ancestors were. It would have been soothing to seek their protections from abuse, and perhaps have more clarity on the perceived lack of intervention that I felt. They could have helped me understand more clearly that abuse had been normalized in my bloodline, and many of them experienced it, too.

I've always experienced a lot of internal loneliness because of this, on top of the varying degrees of trauma in my lineage. Regardless of who was around me, I've always felt very different and misunderstood in a lot of my relationships. I never felt that I had a healthy place to sit my grief, which in turn led me to live with a lot of internalized pain. That pain and loneliness showed up through multiple suicide attempts, hospitalization, immense self-harm, and a lot of self-destruction. I want to be honest and note that a good spiritual life does not absolve a person from struggle or allow them to sidestep dealing with pain and sadness. But it has helped me know that there's always more to my story. For me, being loved across dimensions has given me a different relationship to my feelings of loneliness. They have connected me to better people and severed relationships that contributed to me feeling lonely. My ancestors gave me somewhere, other than inside my body, to store my grief. They taught (and teach) me about the ongoing cycle of death, whether in the flesh or the little deaths I experience when things end in my life. They always replace what is taken, and it is always better. That I am always sure of.

The ancestors are truly some of my favorite individuals to commune with because they do not feel like faraway deities that are too omnipresent or mysterious for the human mind to conceptualize. The ancestral spirits are amazing because they comprehend the many mysteries of what it means to be human. They understand the difficulties of getting up for work, making meals, being tired, and being in love. They are relatable because they *know*, which creates an opportunity for a relationship based on mutual trust and understanding. It also helps that they have the power to heal, protect, and help us access some of the most exciting blessings that life has to offer. I don't know about you, but I could use all that!

## DEMYSTIFYING ANCESTOR WORK

Before we get to altar building, offerings, and some of the other ritualized ways to connect to our spirits, let's consider how to demystify these practices and remember that we don't need to start all this from scratch: we've probably already engaged in ancestor work, even if we weren't fully aware of it.

One of the ways that I like to explain the importance of ancestral connection to those that don't know much about it is that, since I have known and had a relationship with my ancestors, some problems I simply don't deal with anymore. For example, I have a bad habit of speeding in my car, and before I had spiritual medicine and spiritual work, I would get pulled over all the time and get tickets! Now if I'm pulled over, I always luck up with a warning, and if I do get a ticket, it is always dismissed without any points. I am absolutely not encouraging y'all to speed, and yes I *do* need to slow down, but I have to acknowledge the fact that I'm divinely protected and good the majority of the time. I'm not promising you any of these specific realities. You may still be getting tickets and having hard, depressed days. Many people who do this work still are. What

I can promise, however, is that having a practice, one that gives you ways to address concerns, can leave you with a lot less worry and much more information—and no matter what you do, you won't be alone. Ancestral work is a tool among many tools that we can add to our arsenals.

I once felt like a person who continuously had streaks of bad luck. I often felt as if nothing was ever going right in my life. Now I don't have bad luck streaks in the same way. Things that are unfavorable absolutely happen, but it gets better a lot more quickly this time around. I know that I can get a reading and have something addressed, while also getting clarity on why and how this situation is happening. And sometimes the reading is simply, "you have to deal with this, but everything will be fine in the end," which is such a necessary reassurance for me. I love being able to know, one way or the other, because there are already enough problems and things I have to worry about and deal with (ancestors or not). Living this way, you'll be able to cross some of your concerns off your list, which frees your mind to deal with the BS you won't be able to avoid. That BS is just a part of the experience of being a human. It will always remain, just as the past remains.

Those who came before us never actually leave us: that is an honest assessment of the never-ending process of life and death. Of course, we know that everyone and everything must die at some point, and everyone will one day leave the physical plane. In many ways, death is the only process that we are certain to experience, yet it still feels like a taboo and is absolutely an under-studied topic in the Western world. However, when we look to ancient religions such as Ifa, we find that ancestral wisdom, life, nature, and death are all crucial parts of living a full life, one that will bring satisfaction and be thoroughly enjoyed. There are thousands of years of study and research that demonstrate the beliefs that ancestors have a hand in the successes of communities. They were an active part of decision-making and influenced the creation of rules, traditions, and ongoing relationships. This fact is severely ignored and often brushed off as superstition and "woo-woo stuff" that doesn't have a place in a civilized society such as ours. Even the concept of "civilized" is full of inherently racist aversions to indigenous belief systems, depriving us of the centuries' worth of knowledge.

My journey to remembering ancestral wisdoms by studying Afro-Indigenous culture—as well as the cultures, sayings, and beliefs of my own family members—has allowed me to move beyond my own limited understanding of the world, allowing me to better understand my identity. It has given me the courage to create the life that I want for myself, regardless of the ebb and flow of sadness, turmoil, and suffering.

*Resilience* is a word that is often projected onto Black people and other historically marginalized groups, lauding us for our ability to survive through hardship and crisis. We are often subjected to resilience as a default identity, and that unfortunately does not often allow us to be fully realized humans—who are strong, but also very tired, fragile, and vulnerable. My ancestors have taught me that resilience is a learned behavior developed through repeated experiences that have required it. Stories about my ancestors surviving chattel slavery obviously speak to their resilience, but what about those that did not survive? What about the people who took the lives of their children so that they would not have to experience life on a plantation? Were they resilient—and who gets to decide that? Through regular ancestral communication, I know that resilience is one small fraction of who I am, and I have the opportunity to speak to the ones that were resilient . . . or who were not, but whose blood still runs through my veins. Knowing the stories of the past gives me strength to nurture my own vulnerabilities. I get to see my ancestors as more than just resilient enough to endure hardship, but

## ANCESTRAL IMAGINATION ACTIVITY

Hopefully by now you've gotten excited about the good things that can come from establishing a strong connection with your ancestors. Let's keep that imagination going for a minute with this exercise. Read through this paragraph and, once you understand this exercise, set your book down to fully immerse yourself in the experience.

When you're ready, take three *deeeeep*, slow breaths before you start this exercise, to ground yourself wherever you are. Imagine that you are in a calming space. I recommend a place outside that has good memories for you . . . maybe a childhood park, in a beautiful pasture, or even on a beach. Now imagine a ring of people starting to form around you. They slowly begin to appear, wearing long white robes or some kind of familiar garments. You start to feel the energy become supercharged as more bodies and faces appear slowly. There are now about ten people filled with calming, loving energy encircling you. It feels like the biggest hug, although none of them are touching you.

You start to recognize some of these faces, or maybe you do not. Whether these are some people you know by name, it's very clear that you are loved and protected in this moment. The ring of people continues to grow and expand with your continued breathing. At first it was ten people, but soon it becomes twenty, then thirty. The energy from the circle continues to grow stronger but stays very calm and extremely loving. With every inhale, ten more people come to this ring around you. As you exhale, ten more people arrive. Young and old faces fill the space.

Eventually the circle ceases to grow wider, but rather starts to form rings around you. There are so many people that circle around you that it creates multiple rings—two, three, four. The space needs to fit in all these new faces, looking at you, oh so lovingly. Take in all the love and support from these unknown faces. Take in what it feels like to be wrapped around so many people who seem foreign to you but who you know care about you even if you've never met them. Allow yourself to bask in whatever feelings or information may be coming to you at this time. What are you hearing or feeling from them? You can be in this space as long as you desire. Continue deeply breathing as you soak this in. When you're ready to come out of this meditation, keep breathing as you notice the faces and long-robed individuals start to slowly disappear, as you remain in the middle. Thank them and open your eyes.

---

WHAT WAS THIS EXPERIENCE LIKE FOR YOU? WERE YOU ABLE TO SEE ANYTHING?

WHAT DID THIS EXPERIENCE FEEL LIKE IN YOUR BODY? DID YOU EXPERIENCE COLD OR HOT SENSATIONS?

DID THIS TEACH YOU ANYTHING ABOUT YOUR ANCESTORS OR YOURSELF? IF SO, WHAT?

IF YOU HAD TROUBLE VISUALIZING THIS IMAGE, WHAT DO YOU THINK MAY HAVE GOTTEN IN THE WAY?

---

This simple exercise is a way to train your mind's eye to start connecting to the power of the ancestors that are already around you. Oftentimes when I am conducting readings for clients, their ancestors will show up, hovering around the client lovingly and peacefully such as in this visualization we just practiced. Do this work as often as you like to start to better understand how that ancestral energy shows up in your life, so you can visualize the amount of support that is possible.

also as people with depth, desire, and faults. They were strong and they were tired. They were nurses, farmers, and singers. They could have been royals, but I know they were farmhands, midwives, and conjurers. The stories are immense, and I'm still learning them. Some I may never know, but they continue to teach me through dreams, archival research, and my own desires, musings, and talents.

I am blessed to be able to connect to the people who bestowed that gift on me. I get to be connected to a web of individuals who came before me, who made sacrifices so that I may live a little better than they did. I am not the first to experience depression, anxiety, or abuse, and I can commiserate with them because they've been through it. In the same way, I can celebrate my wins alongside those who came before me. I also get to teach them, too, about new ways of being and living. We provide each other answers to questions through divination and spirit consultation, further strengthening our relationship and acknowledging that the relationship is mutually beneficial.

For a moment, I'd like you to imagine a belief system that values your success and the success of your community, and forges paths that connect you to the most favorable outcomes of your destiny. Now imagine having an infinite group of spirits who are ready and willing to support you, and exist beyond the confines and struggles of humanness, which often causes our loved ones to fail us, even when they didn't mean to. Imagine that you could consult with these beings who have some of the best life (and death) advice, know how to deal with stressful jobs, have survived wars, falling in love, falling out of love, making money, having sex, raising babies, and being gay, and are a dynamic catalog of every other human experience under the sun. Imagine knowing that you are connected to these people intimately and divinely. Now what if I told you that you don't have to imagine . . . because you have that? If you are engaging with my words, you have those spiritual allies ready and willing to support you through everything.

## AN INFINITE AND TIMELESS LOVE

Loving my ancestors (known and unknown)—knowing that I have this entire spirit team of people rooting for me—has allowed me to experience a connection that I didn't know was possible. How could I doubt myself when I am made up of cells of all other people before me who made it? How could I speak poorly over myself, knowing that I am a collection of faces and bodies of so many people who came before me? I would never say that my ancestors were ugly, undeserving, or unlovable, and if I am made in their image, how could I say that about myself? I know a love that is not bound by the problems of the world, but infinite and timeless. I get to learn more about the people who surround me. We are always in some form of communication, whether I am speaking to them directly, or if I am smelling my grandfather's scent as I pass an older man. I get to feel their love when I dream about family members after they have passed away, and even when I'm struck by the sense of being home while visiting certain places in the deep South, or even the Caribbean.

Intentional communication and cultivating ancestral relationships have given me the tools to feel more connected to my own body and enhanced the ways that I'm able to relate to others. Beyond the material, spiritual, and financial gains that these connections have given me, most importantly I've watched it heal myself and my community deeper than any other tool that I've ever used or practiced. I want you to recall your ancestral gifts so that you feel less alone, too. I want you to know that you have lovers and warriors surrounding you through all your choices in life, and if you let them and learn to trust them, they can shift the trajectory of your life so that life doesn't just "happen to you" but you get to experience it fully.

I want my people, Black people, to know that our history is more vast than any history book and mainstream media will allow you to know. You are connected to some of the first scientists, beauticians, doctors, midwives, medicine people, and performers. You descend from not only royalty but fishermen, cooks, iron welders, and witches. Someone somewhere in your lineage knows exactly what you are going through, and I want you to feel supported through that. If there's one thing so many of us need, it's belonging, connection, and help. I want us to use all the resources that our spirits laid out for us, so that we can get that help. We can no longer trust that the news, media, and even some of our churches have our best interests at heart. It's clear that our ancestral religions have historically been considered demonic and even archaic ways to live, even by our own community.

A reckoning is happening throughout the African diaspora, and people are seeking deeper connections because we instinctively know that there is more to our existence than what we've been told. We are feeling a pull to something else that extends beyond what has been deemed the acceptable way of engaging with Spirit. And although building intentional relationships with the ancestors will not alleviate all ills and problems of the world, it can help you uncover pieces of your personhood that would be otherwise hidden and unknown. Your ancestors will solidify your moralities, stretch your emotional capacities, and challenge your worldview. They will remind you of your destiny, advise you on your decisions, and love you even when you fail to do any of that. They will exercise patience because they, of all people, understand—although they may cuss you out when you slip up. Even when you make bad choices, they will love you. I want you to know that you are so deeply loved, understood, and seen, and my offering is to remind you of all the people that left you the medicines to deal with the personal, mental, spiritual, and societal ills.

As you do this work, you will be challenged, and you will *disagree*. Just remember that your ancestral spirits want what's best for you, the lineage, and the bloodline, even though sometimes we are just not interested in that. And you have a right to a difference of opinion. In that case, your ancestors will teach you how love can still be present in the midst of disagreement. You will not like them all the time. You may even wonder if you have lost your mind and if you're worshiping demons . . . but trust that you will be understood. And when you're not understood by one ancestor, you will be understood by Uncle Terry or Olotu (your great-times-twenty-five-grandfather). You are not alone.

Your ancestors are not your opps, and you'll learn that as you develop your relationship with them. Your ancestors are not God, either, and they will not make your life perfect, which you will also learn quickly. You'll definitely battle the urge to yell, "Why would y'all let that happen to me?" when something bad happens in spite of the connection you've established . . . and then you will have to reckon with whatever answer you receive (or don't) from that question. I will remind you throughout this book that shit still happens—it's just that if you do this work, you'll have better tools when it does.

I want to quote one of my favorite Bible verses that my ancestors speak to me through, as their way of reminding me that they are not my opponents, even when they're saying something I don't want to hear. It comes from Jeremiah 29:11: "'For I know the plans I have for you,' declares the Lord, 'plans to prosper you and not to harm you, plans to give you a hope and a future.'" I absolutely love this verse because it reminds me that, although I don't know what their plans are, or why something shifted in my life the way that it did, my ancestors have good things brewing for me. In such an individually centered society, one where many of us have developed an aversion to trusting others, struggling with your ancestors and learning to let love in is one of the most pivotal and healing experiences that we can experience. Not to be cliché, but love *is* a powerful weapon. And through my connection with them, I have more of that protection and safety because I'm learning what love actually is. You also have ones that are going to war for you, in every capacity.

# CHAPTER 7

# ANCESTORS ARE EVERYWHERE (BABIES, BONES, AND BIBLES)

My ancestors are my very best friends, and talking about them is one of my greatest joys and privileges. However, I know that the term *ancestor* is very big; it can encompass many people, personalities, and celestial bodies. In this chapter, I will try to make the concept of ancestors as simple as possible, while acknowledging that understanding the specifics of this group of spirits can be a complex undertaking and they contain myriad understandings that must be addressed.

To understand the ancestors' importance, I love to share a story that my former therapist Dr. Linda Robinson shared with me. I was very early in my journey of studying ancestors, Orisha, and other spiritual cosmologies. Like many people newly initiated into the world of African spirituality, I was so obsessed with connecting myself to specific "high-level" deities. I wanted to know more about deities like Oshun, Erzulie Dantor, and Centella Ndoki. These deities seemed more interesting to me! Their mysterious ways and lore inspired me to want to go and set up shrines I knew nothing about. I felt especially close to these spirits and others, and I began to attribute a lot of my blessings to them in particular. Although this was sometimes the case, I was neglecting to first address my ancestral path, since it had allowed me to connect with these deities in the first place. Dr. Robinson, who also happened to be an Oshun priestess, was a perfect person to talk to about my newly developing spiritual journey.

Above all, she shared with me the importance of prioritizing our ancestors before jumping into relationships with other deities.

During one of our sessions, Dr. Robinson politely asked me, "Who do you believe is most important in your life? Your ancestors or other deities like the Orisha?"

"I'm not sure," I answered. "The Orisha?"

"The Orisha are very important," she said, "but imagine this. Say you have a small child with you and you are walking down the street. I run into you and your child and I have a piece of candy that I want to share with your baby. Can I just walk up to your baby and hand them a piece of candy?"

"Uh . . . no. Don't be handing my baby stuff without my permission!"

"Exactly. I would need to ask you if I can give your child some candy. That would be the only way that your child can get some, or you would have an issue with that. Ancestor relationships work in a similar way. Other deities may have blessings for you, but if your ancestors say no, it's no."

I am forever grateful to Dr. Robinson for sharing that information with me, because it really crystallized the importance of being in a good relationship with my ancestors in my mind. If I want all my blessings, I need to make sure my ancestors are allowing me to get every piece of candy possible that I can eat! Or to see that the candy is good for me at all.

Essentially, ancestors are the group of spirits who lived before us and have passed away physically but whose life, love, sacrifices, and intentions still fuel us. In the Orisha tradition, we refer to ancestors as our egungun, but they are ancestors not simply because they died, but because they reached the status of "ancestorship." Yes, to be an ancestor is a title and status that is earned. To make it simple, dying doesn't make you special—everybody does it. Some people die and now they're just dead. If someone who was an absolutely wretched person in life passes away, they do not become an ancestor simply because they died. They probably have a bit more work to do in order to reach that status, if they ever do. To be an ancestor, to be egungun, is an elevated state of being that an individual earned because of their role and/or age. An egungun has been uplifted as a venerated spirit within their community, which gives them the label of ancestor. This communal elevation is such an important reason why our ancestors want to be remembered by families and the collective. Our ancestors want to live on, and they do so through our memories as well as through their connection with the living.

In many African traditional belief systems, ancestors can be "reborn" through their descendants and other people. Think of how you see a baby and say, "They've been here before." That's a way that many Black folks have retained the knowledge that ancestors reincarnate through new life. The ancestors are often reborn again because they have lessons or destinies that they need to fulfill, that they were not able to fulfill in their previous lives. This is why they choose to be born through specific family members—so that they can complete whatever soul mission they may have and fulfill responsibilities that they may have to themselves, their families, and their communities. Now here is where it may get a little complicated. Although an ancestor can be reborn through a new-born baby, their entire "essence" is not necessarily in that new baby. This means that even if an ancestor may have reincarnated in a baby, you may still be able to connect with your grandfather's spirit outside that baby for love, care, and advice.

For example, you may have lost your grandfather as a child, and now that you are of birthing age, you find yourself pregnant with a boy! Your entire family thinks that the baby has an "old soul" with mannerisms that highly resemble those of your grandfather. Based on some African spiritual systems and beliefs, you could determine that the grandfather was "reborn" as your son to fulfill his soul duties within the family. However, just because your grandfather is now your "son" does not mean that your son is not his own person, or that your grandfather is also not present within the ancestral realm watching over you. I know this can sound a bit confusing, but when understanding and relating to spirits, you're not able to apply traditional rules of time and space to them. Ancestors and other spirits can and do exist within multiple realms, within multiple people, and during multiple time frames and generations.

There are also different kinds of ancestors that influence our lives, and it's important to name them before we discuss how to grow in relationship with them. There are blood ancestors, collective ancestors, and overall ancestral spirits (who may not even be human).

## BLOOD ANCESTORS

Blood ancestors are traditionally the people that we descended from, like a grandparent or a great-great-great-grandmother. I also consider blood ancestors to be deceased family members who have elevated to the ancestral realm, regardless of whether you descended from them. For example, if you had a younger cousin pass away, they could be considered a blood ancestor. If someone lost a baby while in utero, that child can be considered a blood ancestor. I know that in our minds we sometimes visualize ancestors as elderly people, because we don't want to lose our loved ones until they've lived a long life and die of old age. Unfortunately, we know that babies, children, teens, and young adults pass away, too, and I believe that they join the ancestral realm regardless of the age they were when they died. Children, just like adults, have their own support, guidance, and insight that is valuable for them to share with the living.

I like to think of ancestors as the people who stand up for us and claim us in the spiritual realm. Sometimes I imagine all my ancestors in heaven bragging to other people, saying, "Oh, you see her, yeah, that's my baby. She got her looks from me! She can run fast just like I did! Well, she learned to cook from me! I'm the one that whispers what seasonings she needs to use in the salmon cakes that everybody loves." In that same vein, when I've messed up in the world and have wreaked havoc on myself and others, I imagine the Creator looking around like, "Now whose child is that, causing chaos?" To which, my ancestors begrudgingly stand up on a cloud and say, "Yeah, that's ours, we've been trying to get her together but she ain't listening right now. Just give her a moment." And the spirits chuckle together, shake their heads, and agree, as their great-great-great-grandchild continues to embarrass them. They are, after all, our spiritual representatives, whose lives are so intricately tied with ours because of the bloodline and connection.

Basically, blood ancestors are the people whose blood is coursing through your veins. These are the individuals whose traits you may have, whether you know it or not, in your features and your personality. There is an incentive for our passed relatives to be reborn through us (or other family members) because of the familial connection. They know some of the strengths and weaknesses within the family and can infuse the wisdom that they gained in the afterlife back into the lineage. This can happen even if we don't have a personal connection or relationship to our blood relatives. This is why, regardless of whether we know our blood relatives personally, it helps to have a connection to them, because they know so much about our family histories, health, generational setbacks, and strengths that can aid us in our everyday lives.

A common misconception about blood ancestors is that you have to know who they are in order to connect with them. Many people feel that they cannot grow in relationship to this body of spirits because they don't have any pictures of them, have never met them, or don't even know their names. This is completely untrue! Just because you may not know certain people does not mean that they don't know you. Have you ever been to a function and someone you don't know (or remember) approaches you and says, "Oh my goodness, you've gotten so big! I used to babysit you" or "I remember when you were THIS tall! How have you been?" And as this person is so excited to see you, you have no idea who they are? That scenario is a little like how an ancestor relationship can work before you get to know them. It would be impossible to know all our blood ancestors! Some of our ancestors' names were never even documented, and pictures may not exist. Some ancestors lived before cameras and some before language and communication as we know it.

As a Black American, tracing family names can be extremely difficult due to slavery and lack of proper documentation of human beings. Names were changed or ignored, people were separated from their families, and documents were lost and stored poorly. But all the archival loss has inspired me to want to connect with my ancestors even more! We have hundreds of thousands of people that we descend from, so release the pressure that you need to know everything about them before connecting with them. Your ancestors are the people at the party who knew you when you were a baby, whom you may not remember. They value you and see themselves in you, because you are them. They see their face in your face, and your quirks in their quirks. These are the people who paved the way for us, sacrificed for us, and who usually did their best.

I do understand that the concept of blood ancestors can get even trickier because not only may you not know your ancestors, you may not have a connection or know your blood family. Maybe you were adopted and never connected with anyone in your blood family. Or maybe you had a toxic relationship with your family that has been severed, with absolutely no desire to connect with them in this life or the next. Let me be clear: it's not necessary for you to connect with any person (family or not) that was abusive, violent, or just plain disrespectful to you. I'm not in the business of forgiving people simply to forgive, especially if those people have never acted remorseful or sought a relationship of healing with you. I've often heard, "What about my white ancestors who were slave owners? Do I have to talk to them?" Again I say that you are not responsible for venerating anyone who forced their way into your lineage. Also remember that the term *ancestor* traditionally refers to someone who earned that title. Now there are some people who choose to build a relationship with their slave-owning spirits as a form of healing in the lineage or even "reparation," but this is on a case-by-case basis, usually for the skilled practitioner.

A later chapter will be dedicated more clearly to those who feel disconnected from familial relationships due to racial tensions, abuse, separation, or other issues, but know that ancestors are still for you, you are not forgotten, and you have hundreds more ancestors who uplift you even when the ones you knew failed you. Trust, they're being dealt with, too.

## COLLECTIVE ANCESTORS

Collective ancestors are equally as important as our blood ancestors, although we may not be related to them by blood. Collective ancestors are the bodies of spirits who came before us, and who have reached the ancestral realm. These spirits have also been elevated by a community and can easily be seen throughout history as people that we revere even in death. An easy example is an individual like Harriet Tubman or Toni Morrison. You most likely are not related to those people (if you are, that's iconic), but we still can channel, thank, and revere them. I also have witnessed the power that these ancestors carry and how they've blessed so many of us, regardless of a familial connection. Blood could not make me feel any closer to the esteemed author Toni Morrison—I often feel her spirit through her written word and stories. She, as a collective ancestor, left gifts for us to help propel our lives forward with more meaning. That is the definition of a good ancestor. Another example is the Orisha deity of Ṣangó (Kawo Kabiyesi), who is the Orisha of thunder, lightning, drumming, dance, and so much more. Although these are natural forces in the world, Ṣangó is also a deified ancestor. He was said to be the third king or political head (alafin) of the Oyo kingdom of the Yoruba people in Nigeria. Because of his respected status that only elevated after his death, he was deified to the status of Orisha. So Ṣangó is both a deity and a collective ancestor who was able to achieve deity status because he was such an important and powerful person. He is probably one of the most well-known Orisha and considered by many one of the most powerful forces. His ancestorship is what was able to make him an Orisha to many, collectively.

As you can see, it is possible to channel the spirits of some of our collective ancestors as we would our blood ancestors. Interestingly enough, we often have access to the words, stories, and lives of collective ancestors even more than we do of our blood relatives. Particularly when I was more engaged as an activist and organizing spaces, I would often find myself and fellow organizers in dangerous situations while fighting in the streets for change. Prior to marching and protesting, we would commonly call on ancestors such as Harriet Tubman to protect us as we fought against state violence. She was an appropriate ancestor to channel because she was a freedom fighter who put her body on the line *repeatedly* for the liberation of her people. It would be foolish to move forward without the protections of ancestors such as her, as we can fight in this way because she fought in her way. I truly believe that our freedom-fighting ancestors continue to show up for the living, protect us, and ensure our safety as we try to create a new and better future for our people. The potential lack of blood connection does not make this healing or protection any less potent. It's beautiful to be able to connect with others beyond those we are related to because, as many Black people know, sometimes we have cousins by love and not by blood . . . but they're still our cousins.

Speaking as someone who channels ancestors on behalf of the living through readings, it is not uncommon for spirits who are not related to the client by blood to show up in the form of an ancestor. Sometimes these spirits are friends of the family, who may not have been connected to the client individually but was, for example, their grandmother's best friend, so they've taken on a family role in the spiritual realm and claimed the client as a descendant. Although I don't claim to know the ins and outs of how ancestral spirits convene, I definitely know that ancestors are not always the people you know, or even think you know. It's about who knows you.

Collective ancestors extend beyond those who have been deified or are popular. An ancestor of yours could be a house mother, a very important figure among gay, queer, and trans communities. House mothers often take in LGBTQ youth, embracing them as parents would, with no blood relation necessary. A collective ancestor may be someone who adopted you, or practically raised the people you know as family. There is a common phrase thrown around, "blood is thicker than water," implying that we are more strongly connected to blood relations than to others. However, this phrase has been used incorrectly over time, completely negating its true meaning. The full phrase is "the blood of the covenant is thicker than the water of the womb." A covenant is a promise or an agreement. Therefore our promises and agreements are stronger than our family ties. If your friends, adoptive family, or collective ancestors have loved you more than your blood family, you are well within your rights to elevate those who have honored their promises to love and care for you. And as I cannot state enough, that does not always include those to whom you are related by blood.

## GENERAL ANCESTRAL SPIRITS

So far we've discussed quite a bit about ancestral spirits and how we are connected to them through blood or through relationship and covenant. Although for the purpose of this book, the term *ancestors* will often refer to human spirits, there are many ancestral spirits who are not human. As stated earlier, ancestral spirits can exist across time, space, and dimension. An ancestor spirit can exist within the ancestral realm while also being reborn and existing in the past *and* in the future. We have to move beyond the confines of our human minds to grasp concepts such as these, so while you're expanding your mind, note that an ancestor could be a body of water, a tree, or the roar of thunder. This can be considered a form of animism, which is the belief that natural objects also have a spirit and are living. Ancestors do have the ability to speak through the elements, but they may also take on the form of animals or anything else found in the natural world. When you think about it, nature existed before the human footprint. Humans are fairly "new" to earth, while water and other resources were present perhaps billions of years before the first recorded human being. The trees, waters, and rocks are ancestors, too, because they existed before us (and I believe they will after we are gone). The power of nature is one of the most important and expansive holders of ancestral knowledge.

To ground these sentiments a bit more, when we die, our physical bodies are often given back to the earth: ashes to ashes, dust to dust. The earth holds the bodies of so many of our ancestors who have decayed into the earth and often manifest again through plants, mulches, and earth matter. There are stories of the Kikuyu tribe of Kenya that say that a fig tree in western Kenya, also known as the *mugumo* tree, embodies the ancestors and thus must be respected, honored, and never cut down. Some of our ancestors died in bodies of water, drowning by choice or traumatically being cast overboard during long excursions as captives during enslavement. The great number of bodies that exist within the seas have created numerous spiritual entities that exist in water. Many practitioners within different Africana-based faith practices honor the waters as a form of ancestral veneration, to connect with the spirits that do live within those waters. Nature is one of our greatest ancestors.

Sometimes we know an ancestor is near because a certain animal may cross our path, or the kind of bird that your deceased friend used to love so much perches itself on your windowsill. You may immediately think of your friend and feel an immediate connection to this animal when you see it. Your friend may have sent that bird as a reminder, or your friend's spirit may reside in the animal that she used to love. The limits of who the ancestors are, how they communicate, and how they manifest themselves are without end and can expand beyond our wildest imagination.

## THE ANCESTORS GOT SOMETHIN' TO SAY

Now that we have a better understanding about who the ancestors are, we can understand the fullness of their beings and how they can affect so many parts of our lives. One day, we may all be ancestors, fulfilling our duties as elevated spirits who want to see growth, power, and change within our own communities. As we prepare to be good ancestors, we must learn from those who have done or are doing good ancestral work.

From a traditionalist West African perspective, ancestors are the key to a good life. They have advice and insights that they would like to share in order to improve the experience of their families and tribal members. Culturally ancestors would be summoned using a specific kind of ritual to hear this advice, which would be applied quickly to the lives of those seeking it. Ancestors were called when there were issues in the village that needed resolution. They had the ability to intervene in personal relationships, quarrels, famine, theft, sickness, and any problem that one could face. The ancestors would also be called in moments of celebration so that their descendants could thank and honor them for their good deeds and allow them to participate in rejoicing at the successes of the village. One such ceremony that is still exercised today is the Egungun Masquerade Festival of the Yoruba people. Specific individuals within the village dress in beautiful and ornate colorful robes and cloth, covering their faces while others dance and drum around them. People in the community watch the masqueraders invite possession by the ancestors. During the drumming and dancing, the masqueraded ancestors address issues and strengths within the community while spiritually cleansing those taking part in the ceremony. They also give messages and warnings to those watching. This ceremony is important because it continues to solidify the importance of the dead among the living.

If you are hoping to gain a more indigenous African spiritual way of understanding and being in the world, embracing ancestors will be a key part in your journey. And once again, although I'd argue that the majority of indigenous cultures held some form of acknowledgment of the importance of ancestors, many had specific members of the community who called on ancestral spirits. Sometimes these would be the elders of the community, as in the Dagara tribe in Burkina Faso, West Africa, or in some cases certain people who had "the gift" to call on the ancestors were appointed to do so. Given the interest in ancestor communication within the past few years, I have seen a surge of interest in developing that "gift."

My journey of embracing my ancestors began in about 2013, and then I noticed a shift and conversations increasing in my generation (as a millennial), particularly in 2016. This was the period when I spent a lot of time in Facebook groups, searching for and sharing this content, including a collection of think pieces that inspired me to seek out more. I began to see more and more conversations about ancestors happening online, and concepts such as ATRs and ADRs began to ring in the mouths of many. Pop cultural icons like Beyoncé were even portraying deities such as the Orisha. There seemed to be a remembering or resurgence bubbling among members of my community and even outside it. Words like *ancestors* became used constantly on shirts, Facebook posts, and throughout the media as Black folks grappled with their identities on the heels of heightened politicized police violence against innocent Black bodies. Quotes such as "we are our ancestors' wildest dreams" began to penetrate the psyche of many, some of whom may not have even considered much about what an ancestor was prior to these events. In my opinion, this was a catalyst for a shift in our perception, where we finally began to open ourselves to what the ancestors were trying to tell us, taking their rightful place in the land of the living.

Again I am not purporting that people didn't start doing ancestral work until 2016. We can't ignore the many people and elders who have prioritized ancestral significance for generations, through folklore sharing, altar building, and storytelling. I only mean to highlight the difference between now and then: the concept of secrecy. Not much is a secret anymore, which has its pros and cons. But before this shift, if people were engaging with the spiritual medicines of our ancestors, it wasn't to be chatted about. Now we won't shut up about our rituals! I know this has some elders in a tizzy—people being so loud about a practice that was once so quiet—yet that very thing has made our ancestral beliefs more accessible. More and more people are crossing over into juju land, and it's because of the power of the media.

I've got quite a few elders who found their way to Hoodoo and Africana religions in the '70s and '80s. They were severely in the minority, and the few who were loud about their practices were often ostracized and silenced. Others participated in what I'll call the "juju underground," quietly embracing the spiritual richness of Black culture, doing works, engaging in rituals, and seeing psychics. Root work and conjuring was not to be discussed but was absolutely something that folks were doing when their backs were against the wall. The fact is that our elders made way for us to be the loud and proud practitioners we are today. The ancestral presence that has made its way throughout various media circuits is a phenomenon that cannot be ignored, and thanks are due to the sacrifices of the elders combined with the openness of younger folks. I was recently having a conversation with someone about how I noticed that my generation of millennials seemed to spearhead the technology-based part of the ancestral comeback, while Gen Z has taken it to new heights via platforms like Instagram and TikTok. In my personal story and in those of many of my friends, it seemed that Gen X may not have had the freedom to always explore alternative ways of understanding their spirituality. I am watching that change, including with my own mother and in my family, seeing my loved ones embrace their ancestors and practices. And I feel like this resurgence will continue into future generations, who will execute new ways of sharing the power of Black spirituality and ancestral magic. And that is how it should be.

Baby boomers were often raised with specific Abrahamic spiritual traditions but may not have had much space to delve deeper into indigenous belief systems—yet many of our elders of this generation know the old remedies, prayers, medicines and "old wives' tales" that were an integral part of their upbringings, in spite of their comparatively restrictive environment. In my case, my grandmother is a very Christian woman raised by Southern Christian people (on both sides), but they also prayed spirits out of people, had gifts such as clairvoyance, birthed babies in the old ways, and knew plant medicines that could cure everything from a bee sting to a root being put on you. This was not separate from their ways of living, and they would never have recognized it as ancestral magic or Hoodoo. It just was what it was, and best believe they were still primarily Christian and/or Muslim people.

Gen X seemed to just be minding their own business until they ended up birthing millennials who wanted to know more about Grandma's remedies. It's beautiful to see how our traditions persist regardless of whatever suffering our people have experienced in the world. I think the biggest difference between how things are now and how they were during the past fifty years is that there is currently a process of naming happening. Certainly we have retained the importance of ancestors in many ways, even in the West, but now it is important to name what we are doing. These old sayings and ideas are not just "old wives' tales"; it is medicine that has been retained via the power of oral tradition.

The ancestors need for us not only to know them, but to listen to them, too. This ever-growing ancestral presence means that there is something very critical happening within the psyche of the universe. There are ideas that will be crucially important to us, that will protect us from the negative forces that penetrate our society. We are gaining more and more ancestors each day, losing more and more innocent lives, and are experiencing suffering that will not end in this lifetime. So we need protection, support, compassion, and ancestral advice. We clearly live in a spiritually deprived society, and I believe that the ancestors will not allow that to continue for another second. They want us to see them, embrace them, and ask for their help as we once did before colonialism designated our practices evil and barbaric. There is a healing happening, and I am happy to be alive to witness the collective remembering alongside my people. The ancestors got something to say, and I'm listening—hard.

## BLACKNESS, CHRISTIANITY, AND WITCHCRAFT

As I often do, I was recently perusing the internet, specifically TikTok, too much and for too long. And, as it happened, one of my followers tagged me in a video that really motivated me to fully express my disdain of the hate and vitriol that is constantly spewed from Black people at ancestral veneration, Africana spiritual practices, and general Black mysticism. In the video, a female Christian preacher was purporting that the increase of Black people engaging in "witchcraft" was a part of the white supremacist agenda to erase Jesus from our consciousness (because Africans knew Jesus before colonialism). In the video, she says bluntly, "I don't know who told us you gotta be a witch to be Black." This preacher woman then continues to reject the idea that Black people needed Black spiritualism and was irate at the idea that more and more people of African descent feel that they are "more Black" because they are beginning to understand Black spiritualism. She continued to call it demonic and impure and said that it was the source of our depressions, anxieties, and why we "can't sleep." A part of me deeply wishes that people would stop tagging me in things such as this because I don't need to see any more Black people yelling at me about a practice that I've watched heal me and others. But content like this reminds me of the deep psychological warfare that colonialism has waged on African-descended people regarding our spiritualities.

There has absolutely been an influx of Black people interested in Africana religions and systems, and part of the reclamation has been understanding our Blackness in new and expansive ways. To learn that juju can heal, that ancestors still live with us, and that a "better" reality is possible because our ancestors left and hid tools for us to use to survive makes one's Black experiences look and feel different. Understanding this information does not make someone "better" or "more African"; I perceive it as an opportunity to gain more information that we would not otherwise access if we relied on the media and westernized Christian doctrine.

To address our preacher friend again, some points she made about Africans knowing Jesus precolonization and before chattel slavery do hold some truth. Some people still suggest that Jesus may have been understood as a Black man based on today's standards because of his biblical description, including Revelation 1:14 to 1:15: "His head and his hairs were white like wool, as white as snow . . . And his feet like unto fine brass, as if they burned in a furnace." Many scholars have debunked this, stating that Jesus most likely resembled a Middle Eastern Jewish man in the first century. Regardless of whether he was literally Black skinned, he can be recognized as an African man because of where he was born. Yet today he would not be understood as African, for geopolitical reasons that extend beyond the means of this book. The point is that, sure, Africans very well could have known Jesus before the whiteness interruption, because Jesus may very well have been considered African. And even if you're not interested in that claim, one of the oldest iterations of the Church, Coptic Christianity, was founded in Egypt around 42 CE. So Africans did know Jesus. And Jesus could be considered a North African man. However, as far as I can tell, Jesus is not my ancestor. The teachings of many popularized and westernized Abrahamic texts do not acknowledge where West and often Central African people fit into the narrative.

Ancestral veneration is all throughout the Bible. I grew up singing about it in Sunday school as well as church camp—a song that we called "Father Abraham." The lyrics went something like, "Father Abraham had many sons, and many sons had Father Abraham! I am one of them, and so are you, so let's just praise the Lord!" This song is meant to teach children about the importance of lineage and the blessings that are possible through the connection to this highly revered Israeli ancestor, Abraham. If you are reading this and you're one of his sons, congrats on your blessings, but as far as I know, many of my ancestors were not descendants of Abraham or connected to the Middle East or the Roman Empires. While other religious groups spread in popularity and culture due largely to political beliefs and control, West and Central Africans—whom I connect much of my lineage to—had highly developed spiritual systems, technologies, and cosmological understandings of the world around them. In fact, many aspects of early Christianity's foundations were laid by African prophets, many of whom were women called sibyls who served as ancient oracles many years prior to Anglo-Saxon Christianity.

As a Black American, much of my ancestral lineage is rooted back to West and Central Africa, most heavily in Nigeria and the Congo of Central Africa. This is no surprise, as the impact of chattel slavery ravished through these parts of the continent as early as the seventeenth century. It is estimated that six to seven million enslaved people were transported to the "New World" in the eighteenth century alone! Of course, chattel slavery had a hugely negative impact on the physical, mental, and emotional beings of enslaved people, but there was also a massive shift in spiritual understandings that severely challenged the indigenous belief systems of our ancestors.

The relationship that Africans have with Christianity is extremely diverse on a country-by-country basis, and even within each country. An interesting example of this is Queen Nzinga, who in 1624 inherited the rule of Ndongo, a state to the east of Luanda populated primarily by Mbundu peoples in current-day Angola (bordering the Republic of the Congo). During her rule, the presence of Portuguese colonizers grew in this nation, as acquiring slaves was an important part of trading and power among many European nations. So Queen Nzinga eventually converted to Christianity, accepting the name Ana de Sousa. Many scholars believe this move was a way to ally herself and her kingdom with the Portuguese and protect her kingdom from falling under Portuguese control. In fact, her baptismal godfather was the Portuguese colonial governor. Queen Nzinga's potentially performative allyship worked for some time, until the Portuguese threatened to overtake the kingdom again after refusing to hold up their end of the bargain and recognize Nzinga as queen (shocking). Nzinga and her people eventually fled, yet Christianity continued to grow regardless of its colonial influence. The conversion of the beloved Nzinga translated to the kingdom perceiving and accepting parallels between Christianity and their indigenous beliefs, including water immersion, visions, and priests with "special powers." This conversion was not necessarily a full acceptance of Christian doctrine but 1) a very strategic political move, and 2) an acknowledgment that ancient Christianity was deeply connected to many African belief systems and can parallel concepts that our ancestors understood and accepted. A new form of Christianity grew and expanded that was absolutely not European Christianity but rather a fusion of practical beliefs that persisted through these regions and beyond.

As Christianity continued to permeate much of the continent through missionaries and political rule, the growth of Islam throughout

West Africa was well underway. Centuries before Christianity arrived in Africa, African Muslims were enslaved and forced to move to colonial America. Traders, merchants, and religious teachers traveled primarily from North to West Africa, attracted by gold deposits in that particular region. These traders brought with them salts, herbs, and Islam. In addition, scholars and teachers from northern Sudan traveled to offer administrative services to many rulers and kingdoms within the West African region. This increased African rulers' interaction with Muslim teachings, which eventually led to conversion to Islam, particularly within the ruling class. In turn, this led to the growth of Sufi brotherhoods, which can be classified as a form of Islamic mysticism, in the twelfth century. As Islam spread throughout West Africa, centers of Islamic education emerged. Beginning in the fourteenth century, West African cities such as Timbuktu in Mali, Agadez in Niger, and Kano in Nigeria emerged as centers of Islamic intellectual learning. Leaders such as the Mansa Musa of the Mali Empire converted to Islam, and Africans found similarities between their indigenous practices and Islam. The marrying of the two created forms of "Black Islam" that still live on today in West Africa and throughout the diaspora. Eventually Islam became the primary religion in certain regions throughout West Africa, and in some ways traditionalists' beliefs were syncretized with Islam. For example, African women and children may have already worn protective amulets for safety, yet after Islam was introduced, those amulets were both worn and carried messages from the Qu'ran within them. Along with this kind of hybridization, Islamic Orthodoxy grew and traditional African beliefs were often silenced and even denounced. Unfortunately, this still occurs, and often violently today as Islamic extremism spreads throughout Yorubaland. This was the case with Tani Olohun, an Onisese (Ifa-Isese practitioner) who converted from Islam, and then was abducted, beaten, and trafficked because of his vocal conversion to traditional beliefs and public questioning of Islam in the Shari'a state of Kwara (the only South West Islamic State). Although originally the acceptance of Islam in West Africa seemed much more tolerable and organic, both Christianity's and Islam's interruptions of traditional beliefs have seriously impacted the evolution of Black spirituality on the continent and abroad, with ancient traditions often becoming a target for anger and condemnation.

Just as with the story of Nzinga and many other African leaders, enslaved Africans in the 1700s and 1800s also did not blithely accept Christianity as "better" because a European person claimed that. It took many years and generations of people to pull the enslaved away from their traditional beliefs. Missionaries would often visit plantations in the South and meet with plantation owners, encouraging them to take a more proactive role in injecting Christianity into the minds of their slaves, both as a means of control and to allegedly save their souls. Initially slave owners supposedly did not care much about spiritual beliefs until missionaries made these visits with the goals of conversion and spiritual control. The Bible was weaponized against many to keep the enslaved in line, encouraging them to do their work well and respect their masters to reach salvation one day.

Although this consistent prophesying to the slave was a form of control, many still held on to their ancestral belief systems and found ways to hide, syncretize, and even fully reject Christian practices. Methodist preachers such as Gullah Jack helped found an African Methodist Episcopal church in Charleston, South Carolina. Denmark Vesey planned a slave revolt and used traditional African medicines and amulets to protect would-be participants (although the revolt never occurred). African-descended people maintained their indigenous beliefs even through mass conversion to Christianity after Emancipation in 1863. However, the relationship of the enslaved to Christianity is extremely nuanced and layered. I think an interesting summation of the complexity of the connection between African Americans and Christianity can be found in Frederick Douglass's words in *Narrative of the Life of Frederick Douglass, an American Slave*, published in 1845:

> Between the Christianity of this land and the Christianity of Christ, I recognize the widest possible difference—so wide that to receive the one as good, pure, and holy, is of necessity to reject the other as bad, corrupt, and wicked. To be the friend of one is of necessity to be the enemy of the other. I love the pure, peaceable, and impartial Christianity of Christ; I therefore hate the corrupt, slave-holding, women-whipping, cradle-plundering, partial and hypocritical Christianity of this land. Indeed, I can see no reason but the most deceitful one for calling the religion of this land Christianity . . .

Douglass's words acknowledge the contradiction that I believe many of our ancestors felt about the story of a freed people through Moses: care, freedom, and salvation resonated deeply in the spirit of the slave, while corruption, the curse of Ham, and the concept of obeying their masters also inundated their minds as a toxic relationship with the Church continued to brew among Black people.

Regardless of whether you were born Christian, we are all impacted by the Christian religion. It is a dominant religion throughout the West, particularly in America where the divide between church and state is, quite frankly, fiction. Black people have been especially affected by Christianity through lawmaking and everyday protocol that often negatively impact darker-skinned and marginalized people. Concepts designated as "sinful" have ballooned and become overused, particularly those associated with people simply having autonomy over their bodies and lives (a concept the West might fear in African-descended people).

Simply put, the demonization of Afro-spiritual practices has been very much intentional throughout history, particularly in the West. From the current use of Biblical texts to condemn people embodying traditional beliefs, to the increase of missionaries across the African continent (particularly West and Central Africa), to legislation in some places (such as Jamaica) that punishes people who practice "witchcraft," intentional demonization of ancestral magic is alive and well today. Intentional colonial rule through biblical means intensified in the seventeenth century, particularly in West Africa, and continued through the 1950s and '60s to the present day. Elder Malidoma Patrice Somé writes about his experience interacting with French Christian missionaries in his book *The Healing Wisdom of Africa*. Somé recalls being taken from his Dagara village in Burkina Faso, West Africa, by Catholic missionaries when he was only four years old and being emotionally and physically abused by Catholic priests. There he was inundated with Catholic doctrine that actively described his family's native beliefs and practices as barbaric. Many Dagara village people assimilated to Christian missionary teachings, perhaps less because of actively wanting to abandon the old for the new, but as an openness to exploring something foreign and interesting for a brief period. It was not until, in Somé's case, he was not allowed to go back to his village despite the pleas of his father that the very real divorce from his life as a Dagara person to a westernized man was highlighted.

The intense colonial periods in the '50s and '60s in West Africa by European missionaries were an effort to gain the souls of African people. Europeans were interested not only in the material resources of the continent, but the spiritual resources, too. The consistent reprogramming in the minds of West African people through the growth of French missionary schools increased the number of westernized African people within their communities. New countries, nationalisms, and other identities came to form as a result of European invasion in Africa, yet the ones perpetuating the "new spiritual ways" were Black-skinned African people. There became very clear divides between those who were taught to sacrifice their indigenous selves for hope of a better future through a Western God, and those who remained close to traditional beliefs and values. European colonizers did not have to be the ones spreading the message and news of the Gospel, for they had indoctrinated many village people, many as impressionable youth, to maintain the teachings of the Abrahamic God among their own people.

Although these stories highlight how the demonization of juju began and increased on the African continent, similar can be said of the United States. Black-American faces, as we can see and feel in many dominant westernized Christian spaces (such as our homegirl TikTok pastor), push an agenda that ancestors, ancestral beliefs, magic, and medicines are the antithesis of freedom building and wellness. They say that these beliefs may even be the root cause of our mental, physical, and spiritual issues within this country. Can someone ask this pastor why people who don't practice ancestral spiritualisms get sick and experience depression, too, if that is the case? How are so many people comfortable asserting that ancestral practices and indigenous forms of healing are the causes of strife that so many people face? How could they say that they are the result of a remembrance and veneration of the people that we literally descend from?

It saddens me that ancestors are consistently relegated to evil, demonic entities. Sure, none of our ancestors were perfect—some of them could have been assholes, mean, and rude. And to be clear, just because our ancestors practiced something does not always mean that it is for everyone. There are ideas that perhaps may not work in this day and age, or ritualistic sacrifices that have no place in our current society. But to call your ancestors demonic and evil is to call yourself demonic and evil. I don't know about you, but my great-grandmama ain't no demon—but I suppose I can't speak for everybody. Let me also say that there are spirits whom you may not want in your sphere. There are entities that don't mean you any good, and really may want to use you for your ancestral resources, offerings, or simply some attention. We are absolutely not talking about those spirits, although how to protect yourself generally is a topic that we will uncover as we delve deeper into the mechanics of talking to your dead.

## MOVING PAST THE GUILT

Whew! You see how intricate, intentional, and long-standing this shit is? This is beyond physical and emotional turmoil; the psychological and spiritual impacts of colonialism have got our people quite bewildered. With all these implications, how is one supposed to start venerating ancestors with the ancestral shame and baggage that is attached to our indigenous traditions? The first step is acknowledging it, and accepting the true gravity of the warfare that has been enacted on our own psyches. Then we must acknowledge that our ancestors, more often than not, tried their best but were also victims of perverted spiritual truths taken on for the purposes of survival. Once we accept this, we can accept that this unlearning and reprogramming will not happen overnight, in one week, or even a year. Peeling back the layers of our spiritual selves and embracing many of the beliefs that were lost, stolen, and plagiarized will be a lifelong journey.

Release yourself of the guilt that can come along with being interested in learning more about your ancestors and spirits. At this point,

I can comfortably say that I know that what I do is not evil or bad, and I'm not going to hell . . . but sometimes my Catholic shame creeps up on me and I start to wonder if I've completely lost my mind talking to spirits, doing rituals with them, and even leaving them food, drinks, and my good liquor. I do sometimes think that it is bizarre to feel connected to the unseen and purport that being in good relationship with them betters my life, but I have to remind myself that those are the lies that many of my ancestors succumbed to. African spiritualities have existed longer than the fictions that were meant to wipe them out of existence, but I do acknowledge that lies, once you've internalized them, can become louder than the truth.

This unlearning will be work that you do for the rest of your life. You will be confused, you will get mad, you will feel like your ancestors aren't listening, you will question your gifts, and you will be suspicious of their intentions. If you've felt any of these feelings, you're on the right path. If for hundreds of years someone told you that you were not valuable—told your mama that, her mama, and her mama, and her mama and so on— you cannot expect to feel like a champion the minute that one or two people tell you that you're special. This healing is bigger than you; this is communal work. As discussed earlier, our ancestors influence a lot of our lives, whether we see them or not. This influence is not just positive, as the negative beliefs that they carry can influence us, too. All our ancestors were not practicing priests, shamans, and juju ladies. Some were imams, pastor's wives, and even atheists. You've got all that history in your bones; the joys and the pains are deep in your DNA. So just relax.

Embracing our ancestors means that we are going to deeply confront internalized anti-Blackness in ourselves, maybe in our ancestors, and potentially in people that we are around in the physical world who won't understand what we are doing. Internalized anti-Blackness is the antagonism against the self that Black folks have taken on because of the severe abuse that has been wielded against those of the African diaspora. Anti-Africanness was the first iteration of anti-Blackness, with the constant subjugation and violence that was projected onto those who were indigenous sub-Saharan African. This subjugation has traveled across borders and generations, affecting those of us who identify as African American and other diasporic groups of Black folks. We will have to confront these internalized sins and projections when working with our ancestors, as many of them passed down these very toxic thoughts that we're trying to escape from. We have to confront the lies of individualism that have plagued us as a society, that simply doesn't leave room for connections to ancestors or even the living folks around us who deserve it.

This is a burdensome role that traditionally would not have been done alone because ancestral work was a communal responsibility. But as we may be separated from our families and communities, whether by choice or by force, many of us are doing it on our own. But is it possible to do this work when we are not surrounded by like-minded people who are interested in doing ancestral work with us? Can we manage this work alone? How can we uncover healing through the long robes of sorrow? These are valid questions. Remember that, by committing to this work, you will be a part of helping the current generation figure that out. And while you *will* be confronted with some of these thoughts, there are resources available to you. While you must not take this responsibility lightly, there are those who will lighten your load along the way. The next section of this book will delve into some of the values that you may be confronted with as you open yourself up to your ancestors.

# CHAPTER 8

# SHARED VALUES

To fully embrace ancestral spiritual systems, one must remember ancient ancestral ways of being, thinking, and understanding the natural world. And while African spiritual systems include a variety of diverse cosmological understandings, there are shared beliefs that repeat values that tie them together. Developing a foundation of understanding in these old ways can help recenter our current beliefs and help us understand the connection between the natural world and human existence, both past and present.

## VENERATION OF NATURE

First note that nature is a key aspect in spiritual connection and healing throughout so many ATRs and ADRs. Many are nature-based practices, which means that they teach that the natural world is significant for all living things, including humans. Conceptually this makes sense: if the earth is not functioning at its full potential, neither can we. Access to clean water, air, and land impacts our quality of life and can even determine how long we can live. Without these resources, nothing else can matter in our lives. Therefore nature is the source that we need to fulfill our destinies.

Indigenous Africans understood this dynamic, initiating rituals to honor the natural world through deification or designating parts of the natural world as deities with godlike powers. Humans were meant to appease nature, bringing favor to the people in their community by taking care of these deities and therefore the energies they are meant to represent. For example, Ọṣun is a river deity found in the Yoruba pantheon, and Sobo is the Haitian Vodou loa (spirit) of thunder and tremors in the sky. Yes, one may honor the shrine of these particular spirits, but caring for the land, not littering in rivers, salvaging our water sources, and respecting storms is honoring our ancestors, thus honoring the natural world. The deification of nature has been a tool used to make sense of its power, yet the power of nature must be respected (deity or not) as the constant disrespect of the earth has been leading to land and water crises around the globe.

## PLANT MEDICINE

In addition to venerating the broader powers of the natural world, many ATRs and ADRs include a belief that plants and roots are highly significant. Leaves, trees, vegetables, fruits, and herbs are all understood as medicinal and healing. Each plant has specific properties that vary depending on the spiritual system, and each can be channeled and used for healing (or harming) by the practitioner. To delve deeper into this idea, *root* is a common term in African-American healing tradition. Roots are the foundation of the plant, found under the earth as an anchor that grounds the plant into the soil. Therefore roots are understood to be the most spiritually and medicinally potent part of the plant in African-American culture, as they are the most unadulterated part of the organism. If a root of a plant is used in spiritual work, it is understood to add more potency to that work. *Root* is also used colloquially to refer to the act of using juju to spiritually harm or control another person. An example of this could be, "John's been acting weird lately and has had a lot of unfortunate events happen to him. I think somebody put a root on him!"

## DUALITY

For many African scholars, including within the traditional Yoruba belief system, duality is an aspect of all life that cannot be avoided. God, the universe, ancestors, and all mirrors of life can exist because of their polar opposites. Up, down, hot, cold, good, bad: all need their converse in order to "work." That being said, there's hardly anything resembling a "devil" or "hell" in a sub-Saharan African context! In fact, the devil as a concept was introduced to ancient Africans largely through European and Arab colonialism. Concepts of an all-knowing and -powerful Creator or God-force do exist, but the difference in these traditions is that, if God is all, then God must include all the good and bad. The only way that a devil could exist based on an ancient African worldview would be if God were all things positive, love, and light. And God is inclusive of that—but not *only* that. Due to the all-encompassing, dualistic nature of God or the Creator, the concept of an opposing evil force isn't necessary and doesn't exist like in the Christian pantheon, because nothing is separate. Of course, there are forces that can be disruptive and cause difficulty in our ability to live an easeful life. However, the presence of these forces doesn't equate to an all-bad antagonistic demon whose main goal in life is to turn people to "sin." Sometimes, it's our own ancestors who may be confusing us, causing discord, or who are traumatized and need our healing (yep, that duality again). This was a huge reset for me, as I realized I hadn't considered how much Satan and the idea of going to hell had affected me throughout my life after being drilled into me as a child. I no longer accept the concepts in my current worldview, and that helps me take more ownership of my own wrongdoings and relax, because ain't no hell to go to when I die. Which is nice.

## COMMUNITY

You may have heard the African proverb "it takes a village" in reference to raising a child or engaging in other difficult tasks. This phrase highlights the importance of community. Community is such an important part of embracing ancestral religions and practices. Traditionally, communities would come together to venerate ancestors and other deities. The success of any individual would reflect on the success of the community as a whole. Communities are not simply people we are around or who have similar traits to ours. A community is a group of people who have shared goals and visions. A community consists of fellowshipping and sharing so that a common goal can be reached. A great example of this can be found in Sobonfu Somé's book *The Spirit of Intimacy*. Here she highlights rituals practiced by traditional Dagara tribes, which were meant to address conflicts between a married couple within that tribe. In the Dagara, the couple was not responsible for sorting out their own issues, which instead became the business of the community, who intervened with the proper tools, prayers, and rituals. If someone were to attend a wedding in this West African tribe, they would refer to the wedding as "our wedding" rather than by the names of the two people actually getting married.

These examples highlight the importance of the people that we are surrounded by, and how their relationships with each other, as well as with Spirit, impact everyone's favorability with the spirits. I find this to be one of the more difficult tools to utilize in the West, as we are constantly engaging with media that underlines individualism as the sole key to success. We also may struggle to connect to others who do not have our same viewpoints and spiritual beliefs, which leads us to a spiritual practice of solitude and even loneliness, which will be addressed later in this book. The popularized Nguni Bantu term *Ubuntu*—which translates loosely as "I am because we are"—can be applied to how we understand our ancestors, and their importance to us both as individuals and in the context of the group or family. As the proverb says, "If you want to go fast, go alone, but if you want to go far, go together."

## TABOO

Taboos are something that are very prevalent in my practice of Orisha tradition and Ifa, but they are also relevant in many African and diasporic spiritual systems and practices. Taboos are specific behaviors that have been deemed spiritually harmful. A taboo harms your spiritual growth and can bring despair to your life if you partake in that activity. They can range from very serious to virtually harmless, yet adhering to taboos is important for aligning with what your soul needs in order to have its best experience on this plane.

Taboos can range from colors that are not good for you to wear to foods that you should refrain from eating. Some people have taboos against being out too late, which protects them from ending up in serious trouble. Some people are not allowed to drink too much because they have a taboo against getting drunk for safety reasons, while another friend in the same religion may be allowed to get as drunk as they want. There may be some general taboos, depending on the spiritual tradition, but often taboos are unique to the individual. I may not share a taboo with my friend who is in the same religion as I am, because our spirits are on different paths. I had to learn early that taboos are not punishments, nor are they in place so that you aren't able to enjoy the good things in life. It is quite the opposite. Taboos are in place so that we can enjoy our lives to the fullest, in the safest way possible. Our ancestors want us to enjoy the good, pleasurable things, and taboos can create discord in our lives that don't allow us to enjoy life's pleasures. Someone may have a taboo of not wearing red clothes while someone else may have a taboo of not cursing for sixteen days. I remember speaking to a priest friend who had a taboo of eating fish. He went out to a seafood restaurant with friends and decided to break his taboo one time so he could enjoy all the fish that he wanted, figuring it was no big deal. Unfortunately, that restaurant was not up to code and the entire table ended up with food poisoning. Sometimes taboos are extremely serious, while at other times your spirits are simply trying to protect you from a tummy ache.

## DIVINATION

Divination is a systemic practice used to foresee future events or uncover meanings and/or hidden knowledge through the use of the supernatural powers or a specific tool. Divination is as old as time and has been used throughout history to understand both the physical and unseen worlds. If you've ever seen someone pull tarot cards to decide if it's a good idea to remain in a relationship, you've witnessed divination.

Think of divination as a mouthpiece for the spirits. I am a huge proponent of African divining specifically, because it gives the querent very clear and direct answers in order to avoid future problems. I can personally attest to how divination has saved me from bad business deals and unfavorable relationships, and has even saved my life. Some common tools that are used in many African and diasporic communities are seashells, bones, animal parts, coconut shells, kola nuts, rocks, playing/ tarot cards, dice, and other fairly accessible elements. Most practitioners within African systems rely on divination to consult ancestors and other oracles in order to get their advice. Through divination, we can best align ourselves with the most favorable outcomes, and receive prescriptions from our spirits.

# COIN DIVINATION ACTIVITY

## WHAT YOU WILL NEED:

Three coins of the same type (I like to use three dollar coins, but you can use whatever coins you have, such as three pennies or three quarters)

A cleansing agent such as water or incense. Florida Water or a smudging wand can work too, if you have it!

## WHAT TO DO:

Step one: Before anything, you must cleanse your divination tools! The coins you are using have most likely never been used to divine before, so you need to rid them of all the other energy that might be attached to them so that they are more effective as divination tools. Cleanse your coins with your water or with smoke from your smudging wand and set your intentions that the coins are blessed and will be used to commune with your honorable ancestors who align in your best interest.

Step two: Now that the coins have been cleansed, hold them in your hands and say a prayer. Ask that your honorable ancestors speak through the coins. Explain that these coins will only be used for divining and let them always speak to you a clear truth.

Step three: Your coins are now blessed and cleansed. Next, I would explain to my ancestors the meaning behind the coins. This is very important. Next, shake the coins up in your hands and then drop them on a flat surface in order to interpret them.

Two heads and one tail: This is what I call a "soft yes" (sometimes "maybe").

Three heads is: HELL YES, BABY!

Two tails and one head: "Soft no," or perhaps another day or time.

Three tails is: CHILE, NO.

Now that you understand your meaning, you will ask your YES or NO question clearly. This is not an intricate form of divining, so questions should be easy. Some acceptable ways to ask these questions may be:

Is it in my best interest financially to accept this new job at____?

Is it physically safe for me to attend this party tonight across town?

Would it be in my best interest to put my house up for sale in September?

Ancestors, would you like an additional offering that I haven't given? (If so, you can list out items and get confirmation.)

Again, this is a very basic form of divination. This method is for simple yes or no questions that relate to you specifically. Please avoid using this to try and pry into the lives of other people without their consent. Do not try to overinterpret the messaging. Be clear and concise with your queries, and allow the spirits to state their claims. As one of my elders once told me, "Divination is always right; however, our interpretations can be wrong." If you're a beginner diviner, keep it simple!

# BAD QUESTION

Here are some examples of questions that won't produce the results you're seeking in divination.

**Bad questions are too complicated.**

Keep it simple! Questions like this will give you convoluted or unclear answers:

*Should I break up with my boyfriend and choose this next person so that I don't have to have this anxiety anymore?*

A better question would be:

*Is this romantic relationship with my boyfriend negatively impacting my mental health? Is breaking up with this person more aligned with my best self? Is this other individual I'm interested in actually a better romantic fit for me?*

**Bad questions are the ones YOU ALREADY KNOW THE ANSWER TO!**

I cannot stress this one enough!! Why would anyone bother answering a question like:

*Are they cheating on me?*

if you already caught him?

A better question would be:

Don't ask, 'cause you know damn well!

**Bad questions are unclear, or too general:**

*Should I move to Arizona?*

A better question would be:

*Do my ancestors support me moving to Arizona in the spring?*

**Bad questions are too centered on others:**

*Did Danielle get her boobs done?*

*Does Julius like me?*

Better questions would be:

*Now, does this have anything to do with you?*

*Is a relationship with Julius one that my ancestors support? Is our relationship most favorable as platonic? Romantic?*

Going to see the diviner is like going to a doctor. They will see what the issue is and use their method of choice to communicate with the oracle. The oracle will state a response and give the client an answer, and the skilled diviner can interpret the message based on their specific methodology. There are a lot of ways to divine, and many forms of divination are rooted in mathematical sciences of probability. Divination does not necessarily involve going to a psychic. One does not have to have a ton of connection to their spiritual senses to receive this information. Again, divination is a methodological way of querying the spirits and must be interpreted by a skilled practitioner. It doesn't rely on the practitioner's spiritual gifts, as much as it is their ability to understand the tools that they are using to commune. Some forms of divination are extremely complex while others can be used by a novice in order to get simple yes or no questions answered. I will share with you a very basic form of divination and how it can work for you. This probability method was taught to me within a Hoodoo context, but it has been used in traditions across Africa, Europe, and Asia. (See pages 96–98.)

## SACRIFICE

In many ATRs and ADRs, sacrifice is used as a ritualized way to give offering to a particular deity or spirit. Sacrifices can be in the form of animal sacrifice, or of time, food, or drink, or through prayer or other means. Sacrifice could be performed as a thank-you to an ancestor for all the amazing blessings they have bestowed on our lives, or it could be a way to petition and appease spirits so that they continue to favor us. Sacrifice happens because we are spending our time or resources in order to appease the spirits, which in turn brings harmony to our lives. Sacrifices are a major part of many ATRs and ADRs and should be seen not as a way to bribe spirits but as a way to acknowledge them for *their* sacrifices—the ones that our ancestors have made and continuously make to improve our lives.

For example, I am a very busy person who always has many things that I could be working on at any given time. However, if my grandmother calls me and says that she needs some milk or a ride, it is nothing to sacrifice my time in order to take care of her. Her having milk or getting a ride to the store is not a matter of life or death, but it does make her happy and shows her that she can rely on me and my care. It may interfere with something that I had planned, but my grandmother has sacrificed a *ton* for me and my family, so sacrificing an hour or two out of my day is an effort to acknowledge that we both sacrifice for each other in our relationship. Sacrifices should be understood not as a burden (although it can feel like that) but instead as actions that work toward bringing harmony into one's life and even those around them. The act of giving and sharing with our ancestors is not separate from the other duties that we complete during the day. Although sacrifice can feel like just another thing on our plates to get done, it must be viewed as the force that facilitates all those other things. Sacrifice is a central part of our abundance, and it is the foundation on which many ancestral traditions rely.

## OFFERINGS

Offerings go hand in hand with sacrifices. They are the time, energy, foods, and more that we are sacrificing to our ancestors or spirits. According to the Merriam-Webster dictionary, an offer is an expression of readiness to do or give something if desired. An offering is described as a thing offered, especially as a gift or contribution. Basically, if we take a look at the definition of *offer*, we can understand it as our expression to do or give to our spirits. It is our acknowledgment that we desire to share with the spirits who take care of us in order to maintain or restore harmony.

Offerings are a great way to appease the spirits in order to reach and maintain certain spiritual, emotional, or material goals. Offerings can be used as a simple way to show gratitude or to reach a specific goal, or as a response to the request of your ancestors for their own benefits. For example, I may want to secure an opportunity for a new job. I have an interview coming up and I want to be sure that I have a great interview and that I'm offered the position. In order to do this, I would like to give an offering to my honorable ancestors so that they can help me secure the position. So I have a few options: I may 1) seek out a spiritual practitioner who will communicate with my ancestors on my behalf to assess if I need an offering; 2) ask my ancestors myself what offerings (if any) I need to give them in order to get this job; or 3) trust my intuition and give my spirits some general offerings in order to ensure the job is mine. Offerings may be given at altars, bodies of water, trees, and other natural sources, depending on the spirits you are trying to reach. Offerings to nature can be extremely powerful and can help maintain harmony between humans and nature. Just remember that these offerings should be biodegradable, as putting out plastics and other toxic materials would be harmful to the land, regardless of the potency of the offering, and counteract their benefits.

If I were trying to secure a job but had somewhat limited resources, I would offer my ancestors fresh water (to keep calm during my interview), something sweet (to sweeten my chances of being hired), and some chicken (because my ancestors like chicken and I want them to have what they like so I can have what I like—in this case, the job). Don't forget to offer plenty of prayer, too! As you can probably tell, ancestral relationships are quite transactional! It can be difficult to understand why your ancestors need something from you in order to address an issue that you may be having, but that's just how it is. Our existence is about exchange, and that's why in Orisha tradition practitioners refer to earth as the "marketplace." Our ancestors do care for us, but we should not see them, or any other spirit, as a source from which we can take without giving them anything! No good relationship should be one-sided, anyway. Our ancestors have needs, too, and the relationship we build with them is not solely about them addressing our human needs. Sure, your Nana may love you, but she still needs a lottery ticket to make your horrible boss finally quit.

Some basic offerings could be:

- Prayer
- Water
- Fruits
- Cooked foods/culturally specific foods (e.g., if you are Jamaican, your ancestors may enjoy curry chicken)
- Liquor
- Tobacco (cigars or cigarettes if they were smokers)
- Honey (to sweeten a situation)
- Candies, cakes, and other sweets
- Coffee
- Candles
- Incense
- A spray of cologne or perfume
- Money (to increase your own money or pay spiritual debts)

Can you think of some other offerings that your ancestors might enjoy? If you knew some of your ancestors, think about what foods they might have enjoyed or activities they may have engaged in while living, and devise ways to incorporate that into an offering. If you did not know your ancestors, ask yourself what general offerings would suffice based on this list.

Personally, I do not offer my ancestors full plates of food daily. On a normal day, their typical offerings will consist of a lighted candle, incense that they enjoy, and fresh water. Do NOT stress about needing to offer every little thing they may have liked—this should be somewhat low stakes unless otherwise noted.

The most important aspect of giving is that you are giving from the heart with reverence and love.

## INITIATION

Across many Africana cosmologies, initiation is a very important aspect of intentionally moving forward within your spiritual and communal journey or practice. Initiation is often a collection of rituals and rites that are performed with the support of other priests, elders, family, or community members that advances an individual to the next level of their spiritual or life journey. Through initiation, you are strengthening your connection to Spirit, the Divine, your ancestors, and your own destiny. It is an extremely serious method that can take days, weeks, and even years. It represents a lifelong commitment to deeper learning and understanding.

If you have ever heard someone who has referred to themselves as a priest or priestess, then they have (hopefully, chile) undergone proper protocol and an initiatory process that helps them elevate in their spiritual journey and connect more deeply to their destiny and certain spirits. Some priests are initiated to help support community members, offer readings, and counsel others as a godparent, while some people initiate into priesthood because it was needed for their health, for protection, or to help their families. Not every priest is counseling and teaching others, and although initiation is very serious, often with standard protocols, it is a unique experience for every person.

Although we often imagine initiations as priests bringing us closer to a specific deity, initiations can happen within families and through natural life events. For example, from a practical Hoodoo perspective, an initiatory process could be involved when a person is finally able to go out with their family members to hunt. As a child, they may have had to stay in the house when the uncles went hunting for food for their nightly meal (yes, people still hunt for their food!). Then, when they were a younger teenager, they were allowed to watch the uncles shoot game and assist in dragging the game back to the house to be cooked. Next, when they reached the age of eighteen, the uncles may have allowed this person to use a gun for the first time to try their hand at shooting an animal. It would be a big deal if this person was successful. When this person first successfully shoots and kills an animal, the family celebrates, probably reminiscing about this person's childhood, when they were afraid of the animal. Eventually, this person may be able to go hunting alone. Although this progression of events may be seen as a normal life occurrence, the process of working toward a goal—in this case, being initiated into the group of "family hunters"—is one that started as a child. The ritual was finally being able to catch animals on their own after many years of learning or "studying" the uncles.

## QUESTIONS TO CONSIDER

DO YOU CONSIDER ANY OF YOUR LIFE EXPERIENCES TO BE INITIATIONS AND, IF SO, HOW?

WHO SUPPORTED YOU THROUGH THIS PROCESS?

WHAT WERE YOU INITIATED INTO?

# PRAYER

As mentioned earlier, prayer is such an important ingredient to any ritual, ceremony, offering, or sacrifice. If we do not intentionally state our purposes for giving or offerings, we're just going through the motions. Prayer is pivotal for setting the stage for what we are desiring—it allows us space to set our intention and define our goal. Prayer allows us to clarify our thoughts so we can manifest our goal through spoken or written words.

Unfortunately prayer is often cast as something that only people who practice Abrahamic faith do, or something people only do in church or in a mosque. Yet prayer is a powerful tool used by many, regardless of religious affiliation. Prayer is an intention that we set every day. Prayer is a form of focused energy and communication between spirits. It can be used to show deep gratitude, praise, make a request, heal, atone, and even harm. Our words have a lot of power, and prayer is a way to invoke that power and establish a clear relationship between yourself and your ancestors. Ask for what you want! And sometimes you need to respectfully demand that situations shift by stating your claims and what you desire. Let this be an opportunity to activate that throat chakra and shift the energy around you through the power of the tongue.

Prayer is a direct communication line to your particular ancestors, but remember that good communication is not just speaking but also listening. Now, I already know some of you all are reading this and saying, "But Juju, I don't hear Spirit, I don't see spirits, so how am I supposed to listen??" And my response is: relax, because you don't need to be a psychic medium clairvoyant Houdini in order to receive information from the spirit realm. Intentional prayer also requires you to pay attention to your body. Do you find yourself getting a hot flash, or maybe a cold chill down your spine? Do you sense that you received a message, or did something specific come into your mind as you were praying? Did you

## HOW TO PRAY

Prayer can look many ways for different people. In my experience as a practitioner of Africana spiritual systems, these are general tools and steps that I like to keep in mind as I pray:

Whom am I addressing?: *To my loving ancestors . . .*

Show gratitude: *Thank you for your love and sacrifices. Thank you for taking care of me in the ways that I see and the ways that I don't see.*

State intention: *I come to you today requesting a job change. It's time for me to be hired in a new position as I'm ready to expand into my career as you would want.*

Make sure you're clear and specific about what you're asking for: *I am being interviewed tomorrow, ancestors, and I pray that the interview goes flawlessly. May my words be clear, may my résumé be the most attractive to the respective interviewers. May there be no other option but to hire me on the spot. And may this job be one that benefits me, my pockets, my family, my mental health, and my life overall.*

Show gratitude again: *Thank you, as I know it's already done and the job is already mine. And if for any reason this job is not mine, I know it is because you are opening me up to an even bigger blessing beyond my wildest dreams. May I be open to all my blessings.*

Closing: *Ase and amen!*

Write a prayer from your heart to your ancestors. Begin with gratitude and let the rest of the words flow. Jot down what comes to mind and try to incorporate this prayer into your everyday routines and rituals. This may be the prayer you use to greet your ancestors or for something else completely. It doesn't have to be long; just let it be from the heart.

hear something or did your cat brush against your leg? All these are signs that your ancestors may be communicating with you, saying, "I hear you." If you did not experience any of these things, I promise your ancestors heard you, too—and I can assure you that they are working on it.

## RITUAL

A ritual is a sequence of activities involving gestures, words, actions, or revered objects. As Elder Malidoma Patrice Somé defines it, based on the beliefs of the Dagara village in Burkina Faso where he was born, a ritual is a series of two parts. The first part is planned by the individuals who plan to participate in the ritual. This helps establish the general process. The second part of the ritual is unplanned, as it is not controlled by the individuals but entirely up to the energy force that is activated through the ritual. As Somé so eloquently states, "Before you get started [in the ritual], you own the journey. After you start, the journey owns you." Rituals in this particular context are not merely routines; they are gatherings where people can express whatever is needed, usually with others, in order to engage a response from Spirit or the energy source.

I have engaged in quite a few rituals in my life—some for healing, some to open paths for more abundance and prosperity, some for safety and protection, and even some to build a stronger bond in a relationship. Traditionally, there is a ritual for absolutely anything. If you are ill, there are rituals for that; if you and your partner are not getting along, there is a ritual for that; if you've been suffering physically, there are many rituals for that. Unfortunately a highly ritualized lifestyle is one that many folks throughout the West have lost, because ritual isn't commonplace. As we engage more with the ancestors in the ancestral realm, we can learn about rituals and their importance in creating possibilities for ourselves and helping us reach the outcomes that we desire.

Although rituals are seemingly less accessible to us in modern life, the desire for rituals is very apparent. Therapists, self-help groups, healing circles, and other clubs have seemed to take place of rituals in the West. Now, I love my therapist, so this is not to say that we should not engage with these supportive spaces. However, ritual adds another layer to our healing and allows us to nurture the soul in ways that these groups cannot always take on. Rituals are wonderful because some can happen while we're alone and others happen in a group. Imagine dealing with a breakup and seeing your therapist to help you sort through your emotions. This is great. You have a conversation with some friends who make you laugh, and it takes your mind off of things. Wonderful! Yet on top of this, think of a space that you create with other people who are intending to engage in a ritual to help mend the brokenness of your heart. There are people who are responsible for tending to the needs of the participants, people who can allow you to mourn and not try to make you stop crying. In this session, you invite your loving ancestors, who will pour the love you feel that you are missing back into you. They come with messages about your strength and the hard lessons that come with the breakup, but there is an unexplainable level of ecstasy and peace that really centers you and grounds you, allowing you to continue on each day. With this newfound energy, you are better equipped to power through therapy and have fun with friends, because you know that there is a force filling you up and helping to piece your spirit back together. The heartbreak ritual could also be a spiritual bath that you need to take for nine days in order to spiritually support you through your grief. Ritual is not a magic show or a trick to make everything perfect again. Sometimes rituals need to happen multiple times to help us properly address a concern, and sometimes they can last for hours and even days. However, they represent a level of healing that's hard to find in spaces that are devoid of spirit building and ancestral healing. Understanding the importance of this way of life will help you understand the medicine that your ancestors have for you, and ultimately strengthen your relationship with them.

## ELDERS

Last, I'd like to share and highlight the critical importance of the elders. Elders in most Africana-centered spiritual practices are the key to ancestral and communal connection. This is why phrases like "respect your elders" have been so commonplace within African-American communities. Elders are honored as life's seasoned professionals whose duty is to guide and elevate those around them. Now this is key. Just because someone is old does not make them an elder. I repeat: just because someone has lived a long life does not automatically make them an elder. An elder, similar to an ancestor, is a title that is earned.

Colloquially I'll hear people refer to those who are wise in wisdom as "OGs." I'd like to think of an OG as a more common way to refer to someone who holds the status of eldership. From an indigenous point of view, elders are the closest connections to our ancestors (besides children). Both elders and children are understood to have immense spiritual qualities because they are so close to the realm of the spirits due to their ages. Although age tends to be a factor, elders are not required to be old people. An elder can be someone who is wise beyond their years or who has put a lot of time and energy into a particular lifestyle or craft that would deem them extremely knowledgeable and an important teacher. Age does not necessarily qualify someone as an elder as much as time, wisdom, and personal sacrifice. It's important to understand the high regard that elders are held in, as this will guide you in approaching and honoring your ancestors. Elders are held with the same kind of reverence you would reserve for your ancestral spirits. Elders also have the last say, even when it deviates from what we may personally want.

Lastly, caring for the elderly—as I've found in my spiritual traditions of Hoodoo and Ifa—has been key in bringing blessings to my life. I've even had a reading by someone who said, "Help some elderly people so you can secure the blessings in your life." That reading was absolutely right. Those blessings come in the form of conversations I would not have had otherwise, the gift of patience, and even a good job offer after braiding my grandmother's hair. I've learned that respecting my ancestors has only brought goodness into my life, even when they get on our everlasting nerve. If things feel a little out of whack for you, seek someone with some sense to commune with, possibly help, and most importantly, listen to.

## FINDING YOUR ELDERS

DO YOU HAVE ANY PEOPLE IN YOUR LIFE WHOM YOU CONSIDER ELDERS? WHAT MAKES THEM AN ELDER OR OG TO YOU? IS IT BASED ON AGE, THEIR STATUS, COMMITMENT TO GOALS, OR SOMETHING ELSE?

IF YOU DON'T HAVE ANY ELDERS IN YOUR LIFE AND FEEL THAT HAVING THEM IS IMPORTANT TO YOU, CONSIDER VOLUNTEERING YOUR TIME AT A NURSING HOME OR HELPING A FAMILY OR COMMUNITY MEMBER WITH A SIMPLE TASK. IT CAN BE AS SIMPLE AS CARRYING SOMEONE'S BAG OR CUTTING YOUR NEIGHBOR'S GRASS.

## EMBRACING THE OLD WAYS

Honoring nature, plant medicine, community, ritual, and elders are all ways that will make your relationship building with your ancestors more comprehensive and clearer. Internalizing this way of seeing the world is not something that happens overnight. In many ways, a lot of these aspects have been disregarded as being of lesser importance in the Western world. Engaging with them will not look like how it did for our ancestors way back in the day. As modern-day individuals we have the power to explore various ways to incorporate meaning into all these important facets of our daily lives. The point, though, is to reignite your ancestral memory of how and why honoring these traditions is important, and how doing so is one of the tools that our ancestors left us for wellness and abundance.

We just took in quite a bit of information. I hope you're not overwhelmed and feeling like building relationships with your spirits is too daunting or confusing. I promise you, it's not. It is serious, intentional, and consistent—but it should also be fun and exciting. You'll soon learn that spirits are wise and to be revered, but also hilarious, salacious, and really just a whole trip. The same way that you know people in the physical realm who are silly, you'll find that you have some silly-ass ancestors, too. Although the practice you are developing is referred to as ancestral "work," know that ancestors give us so much grace as we learn about them and how to commune with them properly. Remember, your ancestors were once humans, so they vividly remember how confusing it was to be alive. Know that as long as you are operating from a place of genuine love and curiosity you'll be fine.

Not only *will* you be fine, but you already *are,* because ancestral veneration isn't something completely new to you. As we've learned already, ancestral veneration is all around us: marathons, streets, and organizations are often named after beloved dead folks. The desire to perfect the recipe of Auntie Mary's sweet potato pie is a form of ancestral veneration. The act of intentionally validating and honoring the importance of someone who has departed us is a huge component of what our ancestors desire from the spiritual realm. They want to be remembered, honored, and venerated—so if you've ever done this, your ancestral journey has already begun. Ancestors want to be properly elevated and remembered fondly. To me, it makes sense to want to leave a legacy. This is a conversation that happens among the living—the desire to be remembered well. I'm sure it means that you lived a good and honorable life, which I'm sure would bring the dead and the living a lot of peace.

Ancestral veneration could also be looking in the mirror and admiring yourself. Perhaps you love your almond-shaped eyes or the dimples in your cheeks. Maybe you love your height or the coil of your hair. All these attributes that you admire came from multiple ancestors of yours. This acknowledgment that you're beautiful because the people before you were beautiful is such a kind way to honor yourself and the gorgeousness of your lineage. If you're from the city like me, you may have seen street vigils and altars lining corners and blocks, usually where someone was murdered. There are usually candles, balloons, sometimes offerings like bottles of liquor or cigarettes, and maybe a stuffed animal if the victim was a child. People attend these vigils to mourn the loss, and the street shrine will often be kept up for days, sometimes weeks, and even months after the murder. Pouring a little liquor out for the homies (at least in the '90s) was a frequent act of reverence for the dead that is pretty common within the African-American community and pop culture.

## THE MAGIC OF STORYTELLING

One of the most powerful forms of keeping an ancestor's name alive is through the power of storytelling. Storytelling is one of the most ground-breaking tools that we have as a society. Griots and oral history are one of the primary reasons that African and African-descended people have any ideas about their ancestors or who we were as a people. Physical documentation was not always an accessible tool and, as we have seen from those who descended from the enslaved, our stories were often not properly documented to reflect the very real racism of the times. Relying on written words and data is a wonderful way to collect and maintain information, but there is truly nothing like a good story. We as a community owe a lot to storytellers and griots, because they are how we have maintained our historical occurrences, family connections, and our spirituality through lore and other means. If you have ever shared a story or recalled a tale that was shared with you from or about someone who is deceased, you've engaged in one of the most powerful forms of veneration. Simply talking about our people is magical. Stories bring people to life, not solely because of a book or movie, but in your own words. Recollecting the time your cousin threw you a surprise party before they passed is a form of ancestor veneration. Recollecting the time you and your beloved homegirl snuck out of the house to go to a party and got caught honors her name. As someone who connects to people's ancestors on their behalf quite often, let me tell you that our people love stories. They love bringing up memories and recalling the past as a way to connect with the living. Know that you can do this, too, to connect with the dead. Keep their names and the stories alive. Remember, the power of the tongue is real.

# CHAPTER 9
# GO BACK AND FETCH IT

*Sankofa* is an African word and Adinkra symbol from the Akan people of Ghana and Ivory Coast. You may have seen the Sankofa Adinkra symbol engrained on doors, buildings, clothing, and signs. It is usually portrayed as a symbol of a bird that is carrying an egg in its mouth as the bird is looking backward. The Adinkra symbol is also represented as a stylized, heart-shaped figure, representing the Sankofa term meaning "to go back and retrieve." Either way, the popularity of this symbol is quite visible among Black communities and further highlights the importance of returning to the past in order to understand the future.

I often think about this beloved symbol as I'm doing ancestral work. I'm constantly curious about what I may need to retrieve from the past and how it could make my current and future life more easeful. When recalling my ancestors, there are so many things that I value about their lives: their ability to thrive, make enjoyable meals, laugh, fall in love, and resist. These are all memories and concepts that I carry close to me. Sankofa can teach us the necessity of seeking answers from our ancestors so that we can avoid repeating unhelpful patterns that may be present within our own lives and that of our bloodlines. Sankofa does not mean wallowing in our past and focusing only on what has already happened; it is more of an intentional peek into history as a way to gain perspective and broaden our present and future horizons. We can never escape the past, so we might as well use it to our advantage.

## SPIRITUAL WARFARE

Much of my work before embracing a more indigenous, ancestral way of thinking focused on studying society, unlearning toxic systems, and facing the social implications of issues like trauma, violence, and addiction. Seeing the parallels between not having access to basic human rights and strained communities is not hard. I watch people fight tooth and nail to get corporations and lawmakers to understand this and make change. I was once one of those people trying to get the powers that be to become better humans and afford their customers and constituents better rights. But at some point I eventually resigned myself to the fact that these larger organizations understand their policies' negative impacts, and that inequity is by design and purposeful. I learned that greed is the common denominator. If people are living in poverty with a lack of resources, of course the incidence of drug addiction will be higher, but their suffering is cheaper than investing in these neighborhoods. Obviously if individuals are struggling to make money, unemployment increases, and predatory loan practices prey on low-income people—no wonder there will be elevated robberies in those communities.

These kinds of societal ills deeply impact all of us, regardless of where we live. However, trying to convince people who do not care about you to care seemingly has not worked—I found that it no longer worked for me. I became tired of protesting and pleading in hopes of affecting a system that thrives off harming my people. I became depressed by the cycle of horrible news, learning every day about a new group of people who were being abused and whose livelihoods were being ripped away from them. My love and support goes to all the activists and organizers who manage to make this their life's work, fighting for change and dismantling corruption. I am praying for you daily.

I found this work to be unfulfilling for me. I became tired of picket lines and marches. I started to dread living, as my work was centered around what it meant to be destitute. I knew that if I was deciding to choose life and to live, then I had to choose what made my spirit feel more invigorated and lively. Although I, alongside the organizations with which I worked, achieved wins through policy changes from lawmakers, internal relationship reconciliations, and other successful actions, they weren't enough to keep me willing to be alive. This existence started to feel toxic and burdensome in a way that I couldn't handle, but that's because this wasn't my work, and it's hard. I know that organizing is important, but it didn't give me a clear enough map to dream of the world that I felt was possible or perhaps already existed in a distant land in another dimension. I think the biggest benefit that organizing afforded me was that it solidified the importance of having community and relying on your people to help you more than on systems that hate you. Knowing that I had someone to call in my community who was a trained medical professional instead of solely relying on an ambulance and its attendant sky-high medical bills—that was beneficial. This awareness of the power of connection pushed me to go through my personal Rolodex of community members to create the kinds of spaces that I wanted to see. It challenged me to think beyond what was presented to me, and often what I learned to accept as a young girl from Baltimore. It taught me that if you don't have anybody around you that you can trust, you need to find you some folks—and fast. It reminded me that we are all we got.

For me, solely—as in *only*—focusing on systemic human violence did not create an accurate representation of our circumstances, nor did it explain why they are the way they are. Please do not interpret this to mean that I am denying what I'd learned and lived. It is imperative to understand the importance of systems and how they impact our personal and communal lives. Rather, I realized that systems are always backed by something. That *something* is what interested me. That *something* extends beyond the individual greed of the extremely wealthy. Although a pervasive and corrupting force, I learned that the "something" I was searching for was much more spiritual than it was material.

From an indigenous worldview, everything on earth is impacted by the spiritual. As it is in the earthly realm, it also is in the heavens. When there is war and discord on earth, there is discord in the spiritual realm. If there is confusion on earth, there is some level of confusion that has already occurred within other dimensions that we are unaware of. This reflection of what occurs in the world, also occurring in the land of the "unseen," allows us to begin to maintain a semblance of control in our own lives. Spiritual warfare is a concept that I've heard used a lot in Christian communities to explain the ever-occurring spiritual battles that seek to destroy and corrupt our earthly experiences. Although *spiritual warfare* sounds like a dramatic term, it does address the idea that there are forces that are . . . if I can be frank . . . fuckin' our shit up. The fight for freedom and liberation is not one that solely involves physical freedoms of the body and land: the freedom struggle is a spiritual struggle.

In many African and diasporic systems, there are gods or energies of war who are highly venerated. Yes, there are spirits that are beauty, peace, and goodness, but there are also ones that embody strategy, violence, and protection. Love and light may be New Age concepts that seek to bypass the very real and often necessary need for anger and action. Because we have a right to a fully actualized and safe life, those who impose on that safety may face the repercussions of protection by that person or spiritual entity. This can be difficult to internalize because violence is often wielded unnecessarily and constantly against certain groups of people. In the midst of this, Abrahamic tradition often teaches the need for peace, forgiveness, and praying for your enemies while Africana systems more often highlight the right to protection both spiritual and physical. Regardless of where your beliefs fall on this spectrum, understanding the necessity of warfare can strengthen our drive to actively pursue the lives that we feel we deserve. I personally believe that there are many options and opportunities for peace and understanding, but as our ancestors knew, and many of us know now, fighting back is sometimes the next or only viable solution.

Since the beginning of time there have been caste systems, class systems, tribal systems, wars, and violence that have ravaged groups of people. In most ancient societies, we can locate the groups of people who were the most powerful and those who suffered most at the hands of those people. Hierarchies are as human as human existence. Instead of trying to address the people behind the hierarchies, I feel much more energized by addressing 1) the interconnectedness of these hierarchies, and 2) the spiritual rationales behind those hierarchies. The difficulty arises when the people within those hierarchies fail to realize that the subjugation of another easily becomes subjugation of the self and all you love. All our identities and hierarchies are interconnected.

## HIERARCHIES

A conversation with an online comrade of mine, Jeremie McKnight, helped me flesh out this idea. He wrote that nature, which is so important in an indigenous understanding of the world, shows us that hierarchies are naturally occurring conditions. We can see this in the relationship between predators and prey, such as a lion and a zebra. One may assume that lions are better and stronger than zebras because a lion can attack a zebra and devour it within minutes. Although this is true—that's the circle of life, after all—it's also true that the zebra's health is of utmost importance to the health and sustenance of the lion. If the zebra does not have access to good grasses and herbs, then it may render itself sick, and then the lion becomes sick. If zebras are a primary source of nutrition for a predator, then that predator's ability to sustain itself is threatened by the precarity of their prey. The intervention of human beings often cause the loss of food sources for animals due to pollutants, human encroachment, and poor agricultural practices. These lead to endangerment of all species, including humans. Hierarchies exist, but the lack of understanding of the connectedness between each relationship is what may one day contribute to our demise as a species. Our existence is inextricably linked to everything around us, which I learned by organizing and studying spirituality.

Hierarchies appear even within the spirit realm, as humans often relegate God as of the utmost importance, while ancestors and other deities seem to be organized based on their relative secondary importance. I've noticed that ancestors often get relegated to a lesser importance behind more popular deities, and thus are often skipped or ignored altogether. This is why this book exists—to be certain that our hierarchal understandings do not mismanage the necessity of all organisms, spiritual or otherwise, and particularly ancestors.

These occurrences lead me to think that hierarchies may be unavoidable circumstances in our existence. If that is true, then we must question if freedom is possible as a human being. Freedom can be defined in many ways, but in a basic sense it is the power to act, speak, and think, free from subjugation, restraint, or hindrance.

As I've delved further into indigenous spirituality, I find myself knee deep in concepts surrounding balance. Balance can be understood as the necessity of opposite forces in coexistence. For example, there must be good for there to be bad, light must exist for darkness to exist, up exists in relationship to down. Each must be present for its opposite to exist. Can we experience the joys of the world without experiencing its sorrows? Would we know what hot feels like if we couldn't compare it with its opposite, cold? The concept of balance helps us understand the stark differences that exist in the world; however, it doesn't always make us feel better about any of it. This has been difficult for me, because does it mean that we just succumb to the devastations of structural violence because "that's just how it is"? No. For me, this is where I decide to not let the hierarchies that *may* be naturally occurring dictate the material conditions of others. If we decide that perhaps our desire for freedom occurs in spirit rather than solely in the physical, we can move beyond the limitations of the imperfect world.

Freedom is something that Hoodoo and spiritualism have taught me quite a bit about. I now know freedom exists, because I've felt it. I also know that it exists because slavery exists, and that duality gives liberation possibility. I know that it's possible to be fully free in one's existence—it can happen because, although I'm still young, I've lived moments when I've felt completely free to move and think and be without resistance. When I've felt this way, I've experienced absolutely spiritual moments. Whether it was through listening to certain music, participating in ceremonies, or while in trance or possession, the common denominator was that I lived an openness that allowed Spirit to take over my body or the ceremony in a way that was free from inhibition and planning. I think this speaks to our indigenous and elder ancestors' prioritization of ritual not only as an escape from reality but as a realization of what is possible when we surrender fully to the power of spiritual consciousness. I've felt the most free and alive as I've connected to the dead.

In order to address the plausible causes of suffering on earth, we must address the causes of suffering in the spiritual realm. Again, our connection to ancestors provides a path to answers. We may give offerings to our ancestors so that they are spiritually equipped and strong to "fight" our battles on the earth and in heaven. We may use divination to gain clarity on what forces are swirling against us, to be better equipped to address them with medicine and ritual. Sometimes our spiritual environment, perhaps like our social environment, doesn't have the resources to allow us to thrive, further masking our ability to break free from systems.

Those who descended from cultures that understood the importance of the spiritual did gain an upper hand in worldly matters. There are numerous examples of how enslaved Africans and Africans on the continent used their spirituality to fight earthly battles. One of the most popular examples can be seen in the Haitian Revolution that lasted from 1791 to 1804. Through these years, the enslaved people of Saint-Domingue (or Haiti) won impermanent independence of colonial rule from France. What makes this revolution particularly interesting was its catalyst, which began with a Vodou ritual in the mountains of Bois Caïman. Vodou rituals among Haitian people have always been not only spiritual assemblies but also political and social gatherings for addressing and organizing against social ills and effects of colonialism. This meeting in Bois Caïman was different. On the night of August 14, 1791, enslaved people gathered from nearby plantations for an intentional Vodou ceremony presided over by Dutty Boukman, a prominent enslaved African leader and *houngan* (male Vodou priest). Also present was Cécile Fatiman, a *mambo* (Vodou priestess). There they strategized gaining their freedoms and were mobilized to revolt against the French. Spiritual and political means went hand in hand as they prayed, planned, danced, and laid offerings for spirits. This excerpt from the official History of Haiti and Haitian Revolution documents some of what occurred, noting, "A woman started dancing languorously in the crowd, taken by the spirits of the loas (spirits). With a knife in her hand, she cut the throat of a pig and distributed the blood to all the participants of the meeting who swore to kill all the whites on the island." The loa of Ezili Danto is said to have been the spirit who accepted this sacrifice, which enabled the Haitian people to have strength and successfully gain their independence. This example, along with many others, highlights the deep interconnectedness of the spiritual and the social, one that our ancestors knew and understood. Many believe that if the Vodou ceremony did not happen, the Haitians would not have been able to achieve the feat of being the first Black republic in the world. Of course, it is worth noting that, although Haitians did gain their immediate freedom, the struggle to free themselves from French colonialism continued as the French continued to find loopholes (i.e., deliberately exploitive systems) that maintained their power through poor treaties and agreements that essentially punished Haiti for winning the war. The continued pillaging of Haiti still affects this beloved country, and some have blamed this unfortunate situation not only on corrupt politics, but also on the acceptance of a Western God that is not their own.

I'll note that, nearing the end of the Haitian Revolution, Black revolutionary leader Toussaint Louverture (a fervent Catholic popularly named the "Father of Haiti") assembled a group of colonists to draft a constitution in 1801 that declared Catholicism the official religion of the island. It is important to note, though, that some Haitian people, particularly those with Kongo ancestry, may have already practiced forms of Catholicism prior to its arrival in Haiti, which may have contributed to this acceptance in 1801. Also, Haitian Catholicism is very different from traditional Roman Catholicism, including the synchronization of loas and saints as well as the incorporation of Vodou practices that eventually birthed much of modern-day Voodoo. The role of Christianity and Vodou in the success (and struggles) of the Haitian revolution is still a heavily debated topic among spiritualists, historians, and Haitian communities.

---

## SPIRITUALITY AND FREEDOM

HOW IMPORTANT DO YOU THINK SPIRITUALITY IS IN ADDRESSING SOCIAL ILLS?

DO YOU THINK SPIRITUALITY SHOULD BE USED TO ADDRESS INJUSTICE? WHY?

DO YOU HAVE ANY OTHER EXAMPLES OF WAYS THAT SPIRITUAL GATHERINGS (REGARDLESS OF DENOMINATION) HAVE CONTRIBUTED TO FREEDOM TACTICS AND ORGANIZING EFFORTS?

HOW, IF AT ALL, DO YOU USE YOUR SPIRITUALITY AS A WAY TO ENACT CHANGE?

DOES YOUR SPIRITUAL IDENTITY OR DENOMINATION ENCOURAGE YOU TO CHALLENGE INJUSTICES? IN WHAT WAYS?

---

Regardless of the debate surrounding which spirits cause what, there is no denial that a God or gods, spiritual entities, and faith have always been strong components of freedom building (and taking) across the African diaspora and even further around the world. Faith is such an interesting concept because it's easy to point to it as the source of our rationales for so many decisions throughout history. Having faith within an ancestral context is crucial because, although you may not always engage with your ancestors in a way that allows you see or hear them clearly, there is trust that they are there.

Part of the process is learning to trust your faith while continuing to trust your senses and the emotions you feel as you work to commune with ancestors. "Feels" are often disregarded in our society, which so often emphasizes empirical wisdom, hard facts, and tangible receipts. Feelings have often been construed as an inaccurate way to perceive the world, even in spiritual spaces. Yet a feeling is sometimes all you may have as you choose to meditate, sing, dance, or pray with your spirits. You may not hear your ancestors talk, but when you're praying, you feel like you're getting a hug. Or perhaps you feel like someone may be trying to get your attention, even if you're unsure of who exactly this being is. You may feel extremely emotional after trying to pray or as you sit at your altar, and I want you to know that not only are your feelings valid in those instances, you are, in fact, computing a lot of the "unseen information" in a completely reasonable way. Your intuition is helping you find ways to take that information and apply it to your life, and that is a big part of doing the work.

## CHAPTER 10

# CAN WE TALK FOR A MINUTE? ANCESTRAL COMMUNICATION

Every single person is called to their ancestors or ancestral practices in some way. Although not everyone is a psychic, conjure person, or priest, the ancestors move in all our lives and seek to grow closer to us through the ways that work with each individual person. Everyday communion is a conversation with Spirit. When the wind blows, it is Spirit activating us and telling a story about the sky or the atmosphere in that moment. The moon phases tell us a story based on the ancestral knowledge that has been passed down from ancient times, telling us what actions are more or less beneficial during each phase. All this is spirit communication, and all of it is something that you've engaged with whether you realize it or not.

I think that the growth of ancestral magic and traditional knowledge has created a kind of glamour around the art. Although these traditions are old, they have also become very trendy as more people start to understand how accurate and life-changing they can be! And I think it is good that more and more people are understanding their ancestral medicines, as I believe the ancestors are working hard on the other side for this. Yet a downside to the constant publicity is that it can make us feel like we *have* to be actively doing spells or workings, and always be at the altar in order to be seen as valuable or even practitioners of this faith. Many of us feel that we must try to read tarot cards or bones to be seen as a better Black person, more connected to Africa and our sense of self. And there is an influx of people publicly sharing recipes, online altars, and other sacred and special tools, which makes us feel that we should do that, too. But I am here to tell you that each of us has our own boundaries around what is proper information to be shared. You do not have to be an outward-facing spiritualist, or *even a spiritualist at all,* to live a good life or achieve great wonders. We are not all witches, we are not all psychics, we are not all priests. Although it can look fun and glamorous to have these identities, the reality is often not what is portrayed on social media. Remember that some of our ancestors were conjure doctors, and the majority of our ancestors sought the conjure doctor. But there are places throughout the world where these practices (or aspects of them) are illegal and can be punishable by law, such as Cameroon and Jamaica. Even divination was punishable in Baltimore, North Carolina, Minnesota, Oklahoma, and Wisconsin until very recently. Every single person was not nor should have been a priestess, working the roots and blessing people in the water. Of course, these practitioners may have been more accessible back in the day, and perhaps it was more commonplace to be familiar with spiritual traditions of their ancestors before the advent of Christianity, but even then not every person was necessarily as active as the actual practitioner themself. We are all called to commune with Spirit in different ways, and no way is better or more important than the other.

---

WHAT DO YOU THINK ABOUT THE GROWTH OF SHARING ANCESTRAL KNOWLEDGE AND SPIRITUAL TRADITIONS IN THE MEDIA?

WHAT ARE SOME PROS?

WHAT ARE SOME CONS?

DO YOU BELIEVE THERE'S A WAY TO MAINTAIN A BALANCE OF SECRECY AND ACCESSIBILITY?

---

## TYPES OF GIFTS

Because of our society, we tend to value only physical sensory experiences that can be explained empirically. So when you tell someone you do ancestral or spiritual work, they may say something like, "So you see and talk to spirits—cool!" This exclamation is quite harmless, as many spiritualists may have this gift, but it not only points to the lack of understanding that we have about the wide array of possible spiritual gifts that exist, but also excludes the sensory experiences that may have more to do with intuition or gut feelings than sight and sound. Not everyone is a full-on medium who can "see the future" and chat with spirits like you would with a friend or colleague. I do know people who are very skilled mediums in that way, but I know even more people who do not have the gift of clairvoyance. Clairvoyance, the ability to visualize spirits or perceive visual events that extend beyond the normal sensory measures, is only one way to engage with spirits. Let's look at some different forms of gifts that I have often come across during my years as an active reader and psychic.

## CLAIRVOYANCE

Let's start with the extrasensory ability that most people associate with mediumship. Clairvoyance is the ability to "see spirits" or events in one's "mind's eye" or in physical form that may not be visible to others. Clairvoyance is an intuitive sight practice that I've seen exercised through the medium being able to see beyond the physical world, which can include entities as well as past, present, or future events; deceased humans; and other dimensions. Some people, such as myself, experience a more intense form of clairvoyance during slumber. Not every clairvoyant can see dead people like you may see other objects; sometimes they may only see the visual in their mind's eye, or intuitively. Some mediums cannot differentiate real humans from dead ones because their gift is so strong. Some people may refer to clairvoyance as ESP, or extrasensory perception.

## CLAIRCOGNIZANCE

The gift of claircognizance seems most common among the readers and psychics I know. Claircognizance is a form of "intuitive knowing" that occurs when the medium or channel can access thoughts or psychic information without any previous information. Claircognizance is knowing that your best friend has started dating her ex again, even though she hasn't revealed that information to you yet. Claircognizance is our brain's way of being in tune with our surroundings that gives us spiritual insight into the events. I think a lot of the women in my family have this gift—they just be knowin' shit.

## CLAIRSENTIENCE

Clairsentience is a kind of intuitive feelings. It is a psychic sense that you may experience when you just feel like you understand the emotions, feelings, motives, or happenings of the spaces around you. An example of this might be a feeling of "something doesn't seem right about going to the party tonight, so I'm not going." There is no presentation of information, and you don't have a clear knowing, but it just doesn't sit or "feel right" with you. This is a form of clairsentience, and I find it a very underutilized psychic ability that not enough people seek to understand or even listen to. I believe clairsentience to be one of the most important gifts that we can have. I think if more people trusted and interrogated their feelings and saw them as valid, we could avoid a lot of chaos. Empaths, or those who can feel the emotions of others, can be considered clairsentient beings.

## CLAIRAUDIENCE

Clairaudience is the gift of "clear" or intuitive hearing. This occurs when you hear sounds, music, words, or communication that exist only in the spiritual or psychic planes. Many spirits like to talk, and someone with this gift may hear their voices, including inflections, accents, and tones. There are of course varying degrees of clairaudience, and one way that I've experienced it is through hearing music in my head. I often hear complete songs playing in my head (often with lyrics) and quickly voice record the music into my phone so that I don't forget! This is one of the ways that I "write music," although it is hardly writing as much as it is recording the sounds that I believe my ancestors and spirits are sharing with me. A clairaudient person may also hear screaming, crying, or laughing, or perceive background noises that can tell a story about the surroundings of the spirit they may be connecting with.

## CLAIRALIENCE

A person with clairalience can clearly or intuitively smell without there being a physical source to that smell. Have you ever gotten a whiff of perfume or another distinctive scent that reminds you of a deceased loved one, yet you are nowhere near anything that would smell like that? This is a sign that you experienced clairalience. Often, when I smell a certain kind of cigarette smoke, I know that my pop-pop is around! Certain smells connect us to past memories or experiences. Clear smell can even aid in understanding the usage of certain herbs or roots just based on their smells. I also believe that people who have this gift are more likely to pursue career paths that necessitate strong senses of smell like chefs, sommeliers, or perfumers.

## CLAIRGUSTANCE

This is such an amazing gift and one of my favorite ones to experience during my ancestral readings. Clairgustance is clear or intuitive taste! I love this gift because I find that ancestors let me know certain foods that they would like as an offering by having me taste them. At one point I was vegetarian in my spiritual practice, and although I did not miss meat, I realized I was constantly tasting chicken. I learned later through my spiritual studies that my ancestors were requesting an offering of chicken, so they put that taste in my mouth so I could make some for them. This gift is really fun when I'm reading people of different cultures because I often experience tastes of unfamiliar spices, drinks, and cuisine not native to me. I enjoy psychically trying new foods and getting to describe what I'm tasting to my clients, who often know exactly what I'm referring to. Clairgustance may also show up as the ability to understand clear psychic information through tasting various foods. For example, if you eat a piece of cake and can understand information about the baker who made it simply based on how it tastes, you may be a clairgustant.

## CLAIRTANGENCY

Clairtangency is the ability to touch objects or others and learn information about them without prior knowledge. Often people can touch relics or even heirlooms and spontaneously gain information about their previous owners, or they take on the "life story" of the object. Remember, everything has a soul or spirit, and clear touch allows one to understand that spirit through direct physical contact. This gift comes in handy around old buildings, which can be conduits for pinpointing moments in history based on the structures' energy. This gift is also referred to as psychometry.

## MEDIUMSHIP

All the above gifts can be forms of mediumship, but more specifically, mediumship is the ability to communicate with entities that exist beyond the physical world. Mediums often communicate with the dead as a means of sharing messages with the living. Mediums operate within the liminal space that separates the physical world and spiritual world and can get clear insights, thoughts, ideas, and communication from the "beyond."

## DREAMS/DREAM TRAVEL

The gift of dreaming or dream travel is a common one that runs in my family, particularly among the women. The gift of dreaming is the ability to exercise one's gift as medium while asleep. Dreams may be prophetic, provide information about particular individuals, and even be a way to connect with spirits and departed loved ones. In our sleep, we tend to be much more open and vulnerable to spiritual happenings, and thus have clearer channels to the world that is beyond the physical. The old saying about dreaming of fish meaning someone is pregnant is a form of intuitive dreaming that points to information one would not have known. My grandmother has seen things in her dreams that I haven't told anyone in my family. My mother dreams of old friends and issues they may be going through. When you come from a family like mine, you can't hide a damn thing. Dream travel is the ability to freely move to other places, dimensions, and even centuries to gather psychic information. Spirits often take us on journeys during our resting hours where we are not physically able to travel during our waking hours.

## TELEPATHY

Telepathy is the ability to communicate with others using your mind. It is the ability to read and share thoughts with others without physical communication. I see everyday telepathy at work when friends call each other at the same time, or when I wish that a person would reach out to me and they do immediately. People who are often connected very closely, like twins, friends, close siblings, and even partners, exercise this psychic gift with one another on a regular basis.

## POSSESSION

Possession, sometimes called "mounting" or being "lost in the spirit," is a special ability that allows a host to be separated from their own body while spirits or other entities take over their actions, movements, voice, and even thoughts. Possession is an altered state of consciousness that often renders people completely unaware of their actions—this is because they are simply not in control while in that state. Although possession is often used as a scary term, from an Africana perspective, it is a common means of communicating with ancestral spirits. There are hundreds of ceremonies (most notably taking place in Africa or the Caribbean) where ancestral spirits are called to "possess" certain individuals in order to bring forth messages to the community or attendees of the ceremony. *Bembés* are common ceremonies within the Orisha communities in which drummers use specific beats corresponding to different Orishas, summoning them to "come down" and essentially possess individuals as a part of the ceremony. Specific dances are also performed and offerings are set to make their stay enjoyable. Bembés are generally very positive experiences, although the one who is possessed by the Orisha may experience some physical discomfort.

Another method of possession is "catching the Holy Ghost" in Pentecostal church settings. This common practice allows people to open themselves to the spirit of the Holy Ghost, which can result in erratic movements and even speaking in tongues. This is a very powerful gift that must be protected and is held in high regard. Some people refer to those who have the gift of possession as mediums, but it depends on the spiritual framework and tradition.

## USING YOUR GIFTS

All these gifts are one small piece of your connection with ancestors and other spirits. Remember that the abilities mentioned above are not a requisite for ancestor connection; there are other ways in which people intentionally work with their ancestors that may include some, none, or all the gifts mentioned earlier. Not every person who has deep relationships with their ancestors even has one. And there are many working priests, elders, and skilled practitioners who do not identify as psychic or carry any of these gifts, either.

Some people are griots, or storytellers, who share information about the past through folklore and historical narratives, intentionally bringing the ancestors through to the present time. Some folks, such as herbalists, work with plant matter and roots to be able to conjure and create medicines through their relationships with sustaining flora, like many of our ancestors had to. Some folks, such as doulas, serve as the entry point for new life, ushering beings from the spiritual realm onto the earth. Their role is to care for returned ancestors as they enter the earthly plane for their new journey. Others use their skills and learn the science behind divination so that they can understand responses from their spirits. Diviners do not necessarily have psychic gifts, but they understand forms of communication through spiritual tools such as cards, bones, shells, or kola nuts. Writers conjure, artists map worlds that they see and/or dream about from their spiritual downloads, dancers channel something greater than themselves to move their bodies to beats. These are all spiritual gifts that can allow us to be in tune with our senses of self, which are our ancestors. There is a saying I've heard that goes "you are your first altar," and I believe that rings true as we navigate our lives as active spiritualists or everyday people, making our lives the ritual in itself.

---

WHICH SPIRITUAL GIFTS STAND OUT TO YOU THE MOST? WHY?

WHICH GIFT(S) DO YOU FEEL COME NATURALLY TO YOU?

WHICH GIFTS WOULD YOU LIKE TO DEVELOP OR EXPLORE MORE?

HOW DO YOU SEE YOURSELF USING YOUR GIFTS IN YOUR DAILY LIFE?

---

As you can see, there are plenty of spiritual gifts, and some that extend even beyond this list! All these forms of communication can help us better understand how our ancestors may be communicating with us. Not everyone will hear them directly, but if any of these gifts stood out to you in a particular way, perhaps that is your clairsentience kicking in and it's time to take a look at how to explore your gifts more deeply. I can confidently say that every person has the capacity to home in and channel at least one of these gifts!

I believe that humans innately carry gifts of intuition and feelings, but they may have been downplayed because of a lack of acceptance for the unseen. This is especially true of people who descended from those who have experienced intense generational traumas, where intuition was not always welcomed or useful in surviving daily life. This had a very real impact on our ability to connect spiritually. When we become more open to understanding the messages and using our gifts, we can better our lives in ways our ancestors could not. In fact, when we believe that we do not receive spiritual downloads from our ancestors or that we are not gifted, sometimes we just have not identified that it's Spirit talking in the first place.

"How do I know if it's my ancestors or my own brain?" is a common question I often get from people trying to make headway in their spiritual journey, and even from those who have been in the game for a while. It's easy to second-guess your intuition, especially when you've got a thing called anxiety or other strains on your mental health that can make it complicated for you to trust the accuracy of your own voice. As someone who has struggled with severe anxiety and depression, my own negative voice can often overpower the intuitive feelings that my spirits are sharing with me. It can be challenging, but it is not impossible. One way to investigate if what you are experiencing is a negative thought or your spirits is to pay attention to what happens after you get this feeling. Do you become anxious and scared, interrogating yourself with more questions and beginning to second-guess yourself? Or did the information simply ring true, coming through without a flood of additional emotion? For example, say you have a roommate whom you need to discuss some household boundaries with, but you're nervous that it might disrupt your relationship even further. On the day of the conversation you have the feeling *I shouldn't have the conversation with my roommate today*. Where did that feeling come from? Are there any sensations in your body? Was it that you were thinking of everything that could go wrong in the conversation, so you decided not to talk to them? Or does that feeling simply feel *not right* or grounded in your body? Although you may not be looking forward to having this hard conversation, you know tomorrow is actually a better day for it, as your roommate is usually more happy on Fridays. Pay attention to your bodily responses first, and then if the potential download comes with a bunch of additional feelings and worries alongside it, that might be your anxiety, sweetie pie!

I've also heard people describe their ancestors or intuition as an "it is what it is" or "I said what I said" energy. It comes through as a strong whisper, and again is not attached to a bunch of anxiety and self-doubt. When you know, you know, and when you don't know, seek confirmation. Understanding confirmation of spirit may take you some time, but pay attention not only to your body but also to what may be going on around you. For example, an intuitive download that you're trying to decipher will come with a sense of *knowing* from something around you or within you. You may feel particularly sure, or the environment tells you that what you heard is true, like a loud thunderclap or a person sneezing. It could be a bird that flies by that feels like a great omen, or someone compliments your hair and you feel a rush of joy. Don't get too in your head about this process; just know that information will be confirmed for you within that moment or later. Spirit wants to be sure that you understand, so the message will repeat itself if you miss it the first time.

## READINGS AND DIVINATION

As mentioned in earlier chapters, readings are great ways to understand the messages from your ancestors when you're struggling to understand their communication. Sometimes, even when we do have strong psychic senses, readings help give us clarity, as sometimes we need to hear a message from another person. As a reader and psychic myself, I absolutely *love* readings, and I find them extremely crucial in my own spiritual journey. Sometimes other readers can use their messages to give us clarity on our own thoughts, and even ideas or spiritual concepts that we may have missed. Seeking a good reader can be such a pleasant experience, and a good reader helps you to feel confident that you're tending to your spirits properly, and can help us to learn to trust ourselves. There are many different kinds of readings that one can receive, and they all have different methods of communication. Some people are psychics, or those who speak directly to spirits and channel their words and thoughts to you. Others may be better diviners, meaning they use a specific tool (such as bones, Obi, and coins) and methodology to interpret the spirit communication. Some people are gifted in reading messages through objects like tea leaves or water scrying. Regardless of the method used, we always have the option of receiving readings for valuable insight.

Readings within an African and diasporic context do tend to come with homework or other prescriptions in order to shift the energies around you for better outcomes. For example, after a card reading from a Hoodoo conjurer, they may prescribe a specific working for you to help your dreams come to fruition. You may need to light a candle or take a spiritual bath in order to reap your personal benefits. There may even be a calling for sacrifice of an animal that the skilled practitioner should take part in on your behalf. Many Africana-centered readings will be sure to give you work that must be done in order to achieve what you are seeking and should not leave you feeling more confused or without the proper resources. My first reading, like many people's, was through tarot cards. Although I've had great tarot card readings from Black readers, if they're not rooted in an ancestral spiritual practice, they may only tell me what is likely to happen for me, and things to watch out for, but not give me any homework. In an Orisha reading, for example, I will hear what is likely to happen, what to be aware of, but also rituals, sacrifices, or offerings will most likely be required. These rituals have their own cost separate from the reading itself. I prefer readings that give me active tools to use, but all readings have a time and place.

Be aware of scammers, who tend to rush to social media to DM you about a "message" from Spirit that they must tell you that tends to come with a price tag. A good reader never solicits clients or tries to scare them into getting a reading with threats of bad omens. Readings typically do require some form of payment, but no one should be pestering you unannounced. It is difficult to say what an average price for a reading is, as people charge based on everything from their skill levels to what their spirits personally request. I've seen readings range from $10 to $300, but I've heard of readings costing into the thousands of dollars. Again, I cannot speak about anyone else's gifts, but use your intuition and common sense to be sure that the pricing makes sense to you. If you are interested in getting a reading, there are a few things to consider in order to be sure you are going to the right person for you.

## QUESTIONS TO ASK BEFORE GETTING A READING

WAS THIS READER RECOMMENDED TO ME? DO THEY HAVE ANY CLIENTS THAT I COULD SPEAK TO OR HAVE PUBLIC CLIENT TESTIMONIALS?

DID THEY SOLICIT ME AS A CLIENT? (HINT: THIS IS A BIG NO-NO.)

HOW LONG HAVE THEY BEEN PRACTICING THEIR CRAFT?

WHAT SPIRITUAL PRACTICE ARE THEY ROOTED IN, IF ANY?

WHAT METHOD DO THEY USE TO COMMUNICATE WITH SPIRIT (E.G., TAROT, PALM READINGS, SHELLS, PLAYING CARDS, BONES, ORACLE DECKS, MEDIUMSHIP)?

WHAT SPIRITS DO THEY CONSULT WITH (E.G., THEIR SPIRIT GUIDES, ANCESTORS, ANGELS, SPECIFIC DEITIES, THEIR INTUITION)?

DO THEY HAVE A SPECIALTY (THINK: GREAT AT LOVE READINGS, OR COURT CASE WORKINGS)?

## DO YOU LIKE THEIR VIBE?

You will not like every single reader you meet, and this does not mean that they are not a great reader, but it does mean that they may not be the best reader for you. This is about your process and your personality. Take your readings seriously. They can be fun and interesting, but having a reading means someone gaining access to your psychic imprint in this lifetime, and that's a big deal! Proceed with curiosity and an open mind but also sensible caution. Trust your gut and do your research, and if your reader seems like they're not for you, know that there are plenty of others out there who can help you!

Last, in the case of readings, it is important to take heed of the information and follow the instructions given to you by your reader. If you have been instructed to take a spiritual bath, you should take it! I always say that the most important part of this process is not the reading itself but deciding what you will do with the information provided. Do not become a "reading addict"—addicted to learning more from your spirits but never putting their advice into practice. It's easy to want to rely on our ancestors or spirits to make all our decisions, but be cautious of *over-relying* on the words of someone else before you trust your own self. You may be annoying your ancestors with too many questions. You don't want to do that. Use discretion on how often to get readings. This can vary based on the information provided, the individual, and if you are working towards a specific goal with your readings and spirit communication. I tend to wait at least a month or two between readings if I think I really need another one, but usually I receive them less frequently.

## THE NEXT STEPS

There is not one way to channel information or hear from the ancestors. The first step is truly acknowledging that you have ancestors and that they have something to say. Whether you book a reading or seek to understand them for yourself first, the information will always present itself to you. This alone opens up the portals to better understand their modes of communication. For example, if your ancestors speak to you in dreams through flashes of images, you may benefit from using a dream journal that you write in when you wake up to channel whatever you remember or your current feelings. The next chapter will cover one physical way of giving your ancestors a portal through which to speak: creating altars.

## CHAPTER 11

# LET'S BUILD: ANCESTOR ALTARS

I like to think of altars as homes for our ancestors within our physical space. Altars across traditions may look very different, but they are all there to invite your ancestors into your environment, where you can intentionally talk, connect, and venerate them. I think altars can serve as a great first step in letting your ancestors know that you value them and seek to build a relationship. It is a space where offerings may be laid and one engages in rituals, prayer, or meditation to venerate and or honor the sacred. The sacred can range from departed ancestors to saints, deities, or even sacred natural elements. Altars can be found across history and throughout various cultures that used them to acknowledge relics as well as call on spirits that carry significant sacred meanings throughout families or communities. Ancestor altars are shrines dedicated to ancestors.

You may have seen altars in churches or during Día de los Muertos, or Day of the Dead, which is a significant holiday in traditional Mexican culture honoring those who have passed. Some ancestor altars are at the bases of trees, some altars are in living rooms or bedrooms, some altars are outside the home on porches or street corners, while some reside under floorboards. Altars can be in shoe boxes, closets, and even in museums. Wherever someone is intentionally putting together a space that honors the deceased through sacred means, there lies the ancestor altar or shrine.

I will share some common ways that I've seen altars built, or general altar construction. Some examples have been pulled from Hoodoo traditions or spiritualist communities. No way is right or wrong. There are plenty of opinions on the correct and incorrect ways to build an altar that all depend on your lineage, culture, location, timeframe, accessibility, and what you feel called to. Ultimately you have to do what you feel is best for your people, and seek guidance when necessary. People have a lot of opinions about what is proper, but they may be a part of a tradition that does not align with yours. This is why I'll share very general rules of thumb that you will need to play around with in order to do what is right for you and your people. And last, as Luisah Teish says in her beloved book *Jambalaya,* before sharing her insights on building an ancestor shrine in your space: "I am assuming that your house is cleaned."

## INDOOR ALTARS

Many of you may be reading this book from the comfort of your home, or you have a comfortable home to go to. Outside work or your daily activities, your house or apartment is where you'll find yourself. If that is the case, you most likely would want to build an altar in the home to invite your ancestors into your cleaned space. Some folks' ancestor altars are in kitchens, or on corners of kitchen tables. Some people have altars in the living room, as it is a central point in the house, while others like myself have had altars in my bedroom, on a mantel, and even in the closet. Your altar can be on a table or on the floor. If you decide on a table, I usually recommend a table that is made from something of the earth, like wood or metal. But if you don't have that, don't worry about it.

Typically, if you have an altar for your blood ancestors, you would not share it with someone like a friend or partner, because you do not necessarily share ancestors. If you share an altar space with non-family, find a way to delineate the altars so that everyone's ancestors have their own space. They love having their own space and may not get along with other people's family (just like living people). Sharing spaces like these could create a confusing energy around your altar. Traditionally, though, there can be family altars or shrines, especially if people are married or share children, because there has been a ritualized merging of families in some way.

Some important items to include on an altar are a glass of water, a white glass-encased candle, incense, a white tablecloth or small cloth, and some photos of the deceased. My ancestors liked photos at first but came to no longer like them, so that is up to you. I've found that the most important piece of an altar is water and fire—your glass of liquid and candle. Especially if you're a beginner, I'd encourage you to set down your white tablecloth or fabric before you put your candle and other things on it.

I like for the glasses on my altar to be crystal or otherwise transparent, because 1) I think it looks very nice, and 2) you can see the water's clarity much better. There are a few reasons why that's important for an altar. First, water is a portal to the other side. When a baby is born, it bursts through a sack of water in order to open the path from the spiritual to the physical. This portal can hold thoughts, feelings, and ancestral memories. When we include water on our altars, we are inviting our ancestors to communicate through that portal, because water can hold their messages. Another reason why we love altar water is that it serves as a cooling agent. We don't want any "hot" or aggravated spirits entering the space, so we intentionally use cool water to bring coolness and peace to the shrine space. Cool water can also be poured or flicked on the ground as a form of libation to greet our ancestors before we start speaking with them. I personally believe that water is one of the nonnegotiable items for an indoor ancestor altar.

Fire is the second necessary element for me during altar construction. I like to use a white candle because white is a calming energy and represents the "white light" that many of our ancestors entered when they departed this plane. In some cultures, such as the Dagara tribe, fire is the element of the ancestors. Fire is a conduit of ancestral energy that gives us passion, vitality, and will to live. In my experience, spirits are generally attracted to fire and perceive it as an invitation to come forth. White candles are neutral and the ones specifically covered in glass or other material have added protection. You may also use a smaller candle like a tea light or chime candle if you so desire. It should go without saying to practice fire safety.

Another item you may include is incense (I love Dragon's Blood, Nag Champa, or a good frankincense and myrrh combo). People will often say that you should have some representation of the four elements on your altars: water, fire, air, and earth. If that is the case for you, incense is a good representative of the "air" element. I've found that a lot of ancestors love "smell goods," so incense serves as an attractant to spirits while holding significant spiritual meaning. For example, Dragon's Blood is a great incense to use for cleansing a space and removing "bad spirits." Burning this incense on your altar periodically is a good cleansing practice.

The white cloth on your altar will provide a base, similar to a tablecloth. Aesthetically it makes your altar space look pristine and nice, but again, white is also attracting your honorable ancestors and gives you a good neutral base for communicating with them. I don't believe that they are absolutely necessary, but I do recommend white cloths, especially to those just beginning the ancestor altar practice.

Meaningful elements from the earth like rocks, plants, flowers, or shells are other elements that you may place on your altar. Ancestors in particular do enjoy flowers, as they are gorgeous representations of life as well as the beauty of nature. Flowers or a nice plant can serve as a good offering. In fact, a plant seated on its own could be a form of an ancestor altar. As you pray to your ancestors and offer them water, you can be watering your plant. This is a good method for those who may find it difficult to build a full altar because of where they may be living. Regarding crystals, I have personally found that they can sometimes energetically confuse ancestral spirits, especially when you put every crystal you own on your altar. Be sure that the crystals are intentionally placed and have meaning for you and your ancestors. If not and you just like crystals, you may want to keep them elsewhere or only near your altar. Remember that this is an altar for your *ancestors.*

If space is difficult for you where you live, know that you can place your altar wherever you have room in your home. Some elders will say that altars are not to be in the bedroom because your ancestors should not see you getting "intimate"; however, if that's the only place that is suitable, there are ways to get around this. Placing a sheet or cloth over your ancestor altar before intimacy is a sign of respect. At the end of the day, our ancestors know very well what sex is because that's how you got here, but there are ways that we can invite them into our space and show respect. You may also buy a small partition that blocks off your ancestral space from the rest of your room or designated area.

## SHOE BOX ALTARS

For some, there isn't a way to successfully build an altar in their homes because of company, family members, or lack of space. Do not fret! Shoe boxes, cigar boxes, or other compact spaces are great alternative altar spaces. They also make great travel shrines! Set up a small altar in or aside a shoe box. You can line the shoe box with a cloth as a base. Place a small glass of water and a miniature candle like a tea light inside of it, and burn small pieces of incense in an incense holder—you now have portable altar space! You can place your special and sacred items inside the box and even add pictures. Think of it as your sacred box that you can pray to when you'd like to connect or give offerings to your ancestors. Again, please practice fire safety, or place candles on top of foil and away from flammable objects. You should be present when your candles are burning.

## OUTDOOR ALTARS

Outdoor altars can be anywhere outside, like on a tree stump, in your garden or backyard, on the porch, or in whatever area is calling you. Outdoor altars tend to be more "earthy," meaning that white cloths and crystal glasses are replaced with calabashes or small durable glasses of water, and altars may be on the ground or in dirt. I still recommend some kind of container for the water, but feel free to incorporate more flowers or plant life into the space. Find a way to demarcate your outdoor altar (try four stones in the four corners of the shrine area). You can always leave food offerings directly on the ground, in a calabash, or on a biodegradable plate. You can sit, pray, pour libation, meditate, and commune with your ancestors outdoors. Remember, our ancestors are also a part of the trees, the rivers, and the soil. Outdoor altars allow us to connect with the greater ancestral energies, and also give us a reason to be in nature, which is medicine in itself.

---

## ALTAR OFFERINGS

**FOOD**: Cooked food, fruits, and veggies, culturally specific dishes, and snacks are great offerings for spirit. The ancestors love when we cook, but purchased food items can also be acceptable. Food offerings do not need to be in huge quantities, and can even be small portions of what you're eating.

The other day my ancestors wanted a half of a turkey sandwich and some chips, but some days they want Sunday's best, while there are some weeks that go by when they don't want any food. Once you get to know your ancestors, you'll understand what food offerings look like for them. Clairgustance and clairalience, or psychic taste or smells that seem to come out of nowhere, can be signals from your ancestors of what they'd like to eat. Food can stay on your altar until it looks dried out, but it should not be moldy. Dried-out foods show that our ancestors have successfully "sucked the life out" of the food, which is a great sign! You can dispose of your food offerings outdoors or simply in the trash.

**SPIRITS**: Spirits love spirits. Alcohol—especially gin, rum, and dark liquors—are common liquor offerings, although other liquors can be acceptable, too. In traditional Ifa, spirits tend to take gin, while in practices of the diaspora, especially those that grew within the Caribbean, rum seems to be widely accepted. If you have Black-American ancestors, they tend to like whatever they may have consumed while living, which often ranges. If you, like myself, descend from some people who may have abused alcohol due to addiction, you may want to be sporadic with offering liquor. There are varying viewpoints on this topic, and you should consult your ancestors around their desires for alcohol. It doesn't need to be a regular occurrence, if this is a concern of yours; however, I usually give mine what they want.

**KNIVES OR MACHETES**: Protective weapons are great additions to your shrine, as they represent protection, giving your ancestors the proper armor to fight for you in the spiritual realm. It's like making sure that your spiritual hittas have what they need in case they wish to take some more direct action in keeping you safe. Our ancestors are loving and kind, but we also have warriors in our lineage who need their tools to make sure everything is running smoothly. Items such as these help them to do that.

**COFFEE OR TEA**: Coffee and tea are both nice offerings because there tend to be multiple people within our lineages that enjoy these things! It's a great way to give something fairly simple when we cannot make an entire meal or don't have resources for something more extravagant. Many Hoodoos like to offer coffee as a way to accelerate prayers to their ancestors. For example, if I am going to my ancestors because I need to find a new roommate quickly, I may offer coffee while saying a prayer to speed up the request.

**TOBACCO**: Tobacco, whether loose or in cigarettes or cigars, is another common offering made to ancestors. Burning tobacco is a way to call on spirits and can trigger ancestral memories. I find that my Black-American and even Native ancestors enjoy tobacco offerings. Tobacco smoke also brings a cleansing and calming element to the space. Tobacco incense, or other incense, is a great offering as well.

---

## EVERY ALTAR IS DIFFERENT

Your altar is yours to create and build as you deem necessary. There are no two altars that look exactly alike because we all have different ancestors with different desires and needs. Your altar will not be able to address every single request from every single ancestor, but it will serve as a general offering space for your collective spirits. Your altar will most likely change periodically as you deepen your connection to them. Some items will be replaced or even taken off your altar as you learn more about what your spirits like and request. This is a normal altar process that should be embraced.

## WHAT SHOULD I DO AT MY ALTAR?

Now that you understand how to build an altar, you may be wondering what you're supposed to do while there. There are many things one can "do" at the altar, but remember that it is a sacred space to honor your ancestors. You can pray, meditate, dance, sing, draw, divine, and whatever other respectful activities you would like your ancestors to take part in. When first approaching my altar, I like to do libations, which is the process of pouring water or liquor for your ancestors. I will take the fresh glass of altar water and name all the ancestors that I can, sprinkling water in front of the altar as a sign of respect after each name. If you don't know the names of all your ancestors, you can add "all my honorable ancestors whose name I do not know, but who know me" at the end of this list. If this is your first time talking to your ancestors, a prayer such as this can help you begin:

> To my honorable ancestors whose names I know and don't know, but who love me just the same. I welcome you into my space. My name is _____ and I am seeking to connect more with you, because I know that you have wisdom and guidance to share. Thank you for the blessings that I'm aware of and the ones I'm not. I pray that your spirits are at peace and that you are elevated to your highest degree within the

spiritual realm, free of all human shame, guilt, and pain. I know that your spirit is present with me, and I am letting you know that I am open to you. I am open to receiving and sharing love. I am open to the blessings of my lineage, and I am open to the necessary healing. Please commune with me, using my spiritual gifts, so that I may understand you more clearly. Please open my path and that of my lineage to continued success, prosperity, and sweetness. May we grow closer and stronger as the days continue. Thank you for your continued sacrifice. Ase.

Each time you approach your altar, you will want to formally greet your spirits, stating your intentions and offering them fresh water. In some sessions, you may say a simple prayer of gratitude. You may speak aloud, cry, and meditate in some sessions, and in others you may simply do libations and say a quick prayer before you start your day. I like to say thanks and put in a request for something that I may be worried about or need. If I'm asking my ancestors to move mountains for me, I will usually go all out with the offerings and spend a good amount of time chatting with them and receiving their advice.

Although I do not hear my ancestors like I hear my keyboard clicking as I type, my gift works through claircognizance, meaning that ideas, thoughts, or words come to my mind in response to a question I ask them. I'll confirm what I'm hearing through divination. You could use the simple coin divination method to do this (see pages 96–98). Have fun and don't overthink the process! Sometimes the offering is turning on some good music and dancing in front of your altar to some Frankie Beverly, gospel, or West African drumming. Your ancestors were people, so they enjoy many of the things that we do! I have written poetry and even sung to them. Just be sure that you keep up a schedule of visiting your spirits. Is there a day of the week where you have ten to twenty minutes to sit at your ancestor altar? Some ancestor sessions have run up to a couple hours for me, while some are around five minutes long. As long as you address your ancestors regularly, even just saying good morning and hello as you pass them, makes such a big difference.

Please remember to keep your altar clean and refreshed. Trust me when I say I understand that life happens, but you don't want your altar to get crusty and dusty! Be aware of dust collecting on your shrine, wash your cloths if you have them, and clean your space periodically. Your water should never be cloudy, moldy, or have rings around it. Be aware of dead flies or gnats that may have gotten into your offerings. Throw away moldy foods, as your ancestors should not be eating mold. Take care of the space as you would for any respected elder. We invited our ancestors into space, so we should take care of them. In my opinion, if you are not able to maintain your altar without it becoming dusty or moldy, you may want to think about having a smaller, more maintainable altar, or building an altar later, when you know you can keep it up. Again, you always have the option of an outdoor space such as the base of a tree, or a small travel-sized altar.

Although we can easily feel like maintaining our ancestral space is a chore, it is simply us taking care of them and inviting them to work with us. It can be easy to put a lot of pressure on ourselves when we haven't made them an offering in some time—we forget that we are literally in relationship with spirits that love us. But if any group of spirits understand what it means to be overtaken by "life," it's the ancestors. They were human and had children, jobs, and entire lives that they needed to tend to. Although altars are important for us to maintain properly, they understand that we do not always have the time for big offerings and long prayer sessions. We can speak to our ancestors anywhere—not only at our altars—so say hi to them and give them gratitude throughout your day. That is also a meaningful way to let them know that you care, yet you're tending to life. When you have time, though, be sure to check in on the altar space so that you may continue to grow in your gifts and relationship. Taking time for yourself and your own spirituality is always important, as that assists us in our everyday life duties.

I cannot stress enough how often I come into contact with people who 1) are afraid to build their altar because they want it absolutely perfect, or 2) do not maintain their altars because they feel like they've been "slacking" and thus their ancestors are mad at them. Your altar space is not meant to be perfect: it is meant to bring you and your family healing and spiritual communications. Your ancestors are not mad at you for living your life—just be honest and clear about your intentions, follow through on your commitments, and when you cannot, simply say that. They work with us all the time. Be aware of projecting thoughts and feelings onto your ancestors that actually are your own. For example, you may think, *My ancestors are mad at me because I haven't refreshed their water in weeks because of my depression*, when in fact your ancestors only want a moment to love you up and understand your current difficulties. You may be mad or disappointed in yourself, but be careful of projecting that feeling onto them. I'm guilty of this, and working through those kinds of projections is such a big part of my own journey. Do not judge yourself for wherever you find yourself on yours. Consistency with good communication via honesty will take you very far. Do what you can.

You may also feel like your connection to your ancestors isn't strong. Perhaps you don't feel the energizing effect that you anticipated while going to your altar. This is okay! Just because you don't feel like anyone is listening to you does not mean that your ancestors are not listening! They are always listening. If you do feel like there may be a breach in communication, consider questions like, "Are my ancestors communicating with me in a different way?" or "Have they communicated with me but I never listen?" or "Are they requesting help from me?" or maybe "Am I relying too much on the spiritual side of things and not using their insights to do what is necessary?" Ask yourself these questions as you decipher your ancestral connection and relationship. Revisit the chapter on gifts, and know that for clarity you can always receive a divination from a trusted practitioner.

# SPIRITUAL CHECKLIST

Honestly think through your schedule, capacity, current life happenings, etc., and decide on one or two things that you can do each week for your ancestors. Take a look at this list, which contains some options that may work for you. Then ask yourself if there is a specific time of day or day of the week, about ten to twenty minutes, when you can sit at your ancestor altar. Put it on your calendar if you need to, or otherwise commit to performing this action and taking this time regularly.

## ARE YOU ABLE TO:

Refresh their water today?

Pour libation?

Light their ancestor candle?

Light some incense?

Say a prayer for yourself, your ancestors, and others?

Give them a fresh snack or food offering?

Make them coffee?

Buy them a treat?

Play them a song they'd like?

Pull cards or some other divination method?

Sit and meditate?

Dance with them?

Sing them a song?

Then check in with your spirits periodically to see if you need to address any of these necessary steps:

**DO I NEED TO:**

Clean the altar?

Add or take off any items?

Clean the room where the altar sits?

Check in about something happening in my life?

Address any familial issues?

Move the altar into a different room?

These questions will give you a framework for beginning the physical aspects of your practice by working with your altar.

# CHAPTER 12

# HEALING FAMILY LINES

I am so grateful to my ancestors for the wisdom that they have imparted and continue to impart to me daily. But connecting with one's ancestors is not just a solo project—it is one that involves community and especially family. Traditionally ancestor veneration includes rituals conducted by a clan or family unit, and each clan had specific ancestors that they consulted with regularly. Someone would usually be appointed, such as the eldest uncle, to consult the ancestors, leave offerings on behalf of the clan, and appease the spirits in whatever way was necessary. This is of course a bit different today, given that many families live far from each other, are less likely to have access to ancestral knowledge, and may not even know the names of the deceased whom they could benefit from contacting. Family units and communities are also sometimes the source of trauma, pain, abuse, and separation, which can make this process all the more complex.

## WHAT IF MY FAMILY ISN'T INTO ALL THIS?

In a postcolonial world, our connections to our families have shifted greatly. We no longer live in compounds and often are not in close proximity to our family, so how do we go about performing family ancestral veneration now? My auntie doesn't even believe in dead people, so how am I supposed to talk about spirits with her, or with other people in my family who would see what I'm doing as evil? How can I connect to a bunch of dead people whose names I don't even know, when my family doesn't even talk about our ancestors? These are all questions that

I've heard and also that I've asked myself on my journey. Over time I've learned that ancestral connection will not look how it looked hundreds of years ago. It will not look like how it looked for my ancestors who were born in villages in West and Central Africa. It also may not look the same as it did twenty years ago! Family dynamics won't even look like how they did for my mama, who grew up sleeping in the same bed as her grandmother, a room over from her parents, siblings, sister-in-law, nephews, and elders—all living under one roof. It will look like it will today, and that is just as valid and still effective.

The word *family* comes with a lot of notions that I recognize vary for many people. Some people have beautiful relationships with their families: there is closeness, love, and trust. Others may have very difficult and even traumatic familial connections, with no desire to connect or rekindle any form of relationship. Some of us have family members we don't even know physically, or have created new families that we prefer to our original ones. Whatever the case may be, family is a huge part of not only who we are, but who we strive to be. We don't have to live in a village to do the family work.

Start right where you are when it comes to your relationship with your ancestors. This can be a point of controversy, but everybody in your family doesn't have to understand or even know that you've embarked on an ancestral journey, at least not initially. It's okay if they have their own belief systems that vary greatly from yours. Iya Sope, a local Baltimore Ọṣun priestess, said something once that stuck with me: "Your ancestral relationship is very personal, and really nobody else's business." Although this could vary from the original intent of ancestral connection, our daily lives vary greatly in almost every single aspect.

We do not have to share our practices with people who shame us or who seem committed to misunderstanding us. If you feel called to set up an altar, pour water at the base of a tree, or honor the river, that is your business. Of course, you may always ask your ancestors to change the hearts of those around you, and they will, but your practice is yours *first.* Next I'll say that your family probably has engaged in ancestral veneration and even Hoodoo. They may have said things like "Don't sweep my feet, that's not good luck." They may engage in rituals like "Only Lexy makes the poundcake, because she makes it just like Pop-Pop used to," or maybe someone has a place in their home with pictures of their deceased family members with a small candle or flowers next to it (hello, that's an altar), or even says things like "I had a dream that cousin T came to visit me; he said he's all right." These are all examples of the mystics moving through your families and the ancestors' gifts remaining continuously at play. If you're reading this and you're thinking, *I truly don't think my family does any of this,* I'm here to tell you that you're most likely wrong. You are probably simply a part of a clan who doesn't talk about their psychic proclivities, which is quite normal. I guarantee you've got some spiritual folks around you who have prophetic dreams, get very strong gut feelings, and even some who still commune with their dead loved ones. It doesn't matter what their beliefs currently are—none of that has anything to do with your ancestors. You are not the only one to have gifts in your lineage and you have these feelings because someone else in your lineage had them, too. Don't worry about who that was, but know that the gift was passed down and it went to more people than you. I promise.

## SHOULD I VENERATE MY RELIGIOUS ANCESTORS?

I know you may also be thinking something like, *if my ancestors were very strict Muslims, do they want me to venerate them? What if they do not agree with my current practices?* In my experience, regardless of the religious affiliation of your departed loved ones, they do not mind you venerating them. They are dead now, and they have most likely gone through their own process of understanding, realizing slowly that they can communicate and even hear your prayers, wants, and desires. However, oftentimes these ancestors who were devout in their religion will use that religion to communicate with you further. Although you may no longer read the Qur'an or identify as Muslim, your nana may be trying to communicate messages to you through that text because that is what she knows and understands. You can always use these texts as tools for insight and wisdom, while leaving behind the things you may not jibe with, simply to enhance your ancestral connection. Also remember that considering our ancestors to be only people that knew us in life or that we vaguely recall may seem easiest, but we have plenty more ancestors to work with. If you're still healing your relationship with religion, know that there are other spirits who didn't practice that religion within your lineage. Everybody wasn't Muslim, everybody wasn't Christian, everybody wasn't anything. Our spirits are diverse and we should see them as such. Ask your ancestors, "Hi, can you communicate with me through other texts that are not religious?" or "Can you communicate more through repeating numbers, or dreams?" They may or may not honor your request, but you can definitely ask. If not, call on the ones who are more open about spirituality, and understand that there are many ways to connect with you. They'll come, too, but don't throw the baby out with the bathwater. My opinion is that if Grandma is trying to bless you, but needs you to read Psalm 130 for three days with a white candle—chile, pull that Bible out and get your blessings. But it's your call to make, and if religion is traumatic for you and prevents you from keeping the channels of communication open with your ancestors, it's your prerogative to either direct that person to reach out to you in a different way, or to shift your practice to focus on other spirits.

## SHOULD I COMMUNICATE WITH PEOPLE I DIDN'T LIKE?

Remember that not every person who dies is automatically an ancestor worthy of your reverence or veneration. Some people who are now ancestors treated us or other people horribly while they were living. Why would I want to talk in death to my grandfather who was a raging abusive alcoholic in life? Again I'll say that you do not have to. You have the right to open your heart to those who make you feel safe, and if Grandpa didn't do that, that's okay.

The ancestral realm is so interesting because I believe that a lot goes on when our people die. Many elders have shared that, when our people die, they are required to sit and watch their life play out like a movie, including their celebrations and joys, as well as their messed-up decisions. Once that movie is over, a choice is made, not if they are going to heaven or hell . . . but if they ascend to the ancestral realm (to help support their families or others to course correct) or need to return as a human again (also to help themselves and their families) by being reborn, most likely through their own lineage to course correct in the flesh. Of course no one actually knows what happens after we die, but this is how I like to view the end of life, and based on my conversations with the dead, it does happen something like this. Interestingly, our ancestors often don't like a lot of the choices they made in their personal movies, and now that they have better clarity, understanding, or maybe even just resources . . . they can be a better family member than they were as a human. So sometimes that raging alcoholic granddaddy is actually the spirit guide closest to you because he wants to right his wrongs. Not always, but in my case of working with the dead, I have found that many people who were harmful in life are apologetic and want to make things right. But letting them do that is totally up to you. Maybe a part of your ancestor's journey is coming to the realization that you can't ruin your family and expect forgiveness from your descendants. Let them have their journey, and trust yours.

You do not have to know your family in order to know your ancestors. Remember, they probably know you better than you know them. If you do not like your immediate family, that's fine, but that has nothing to do with the thousands of other people that you descend from on both sides. Through divination and even personal connection, your ancestors can even help give you insights into the living in order to bring healing to your family, even if that healing is establishing your boundaries to no longer associate with them anymore. That's also good juju.

Someone I interviewed recently talked about how her family is very Christian and absolutely does not agree with her identification as a "witch" or even a healer (even though her family has gifts of sight and healing, too). She said that although she doesn't speak directly to her family about her witchy ways, she has noticed a change in her family dynamics because *she* has changed. Now that she has identified a deep impermeable love surrounding her, she has been able to be in relationships with her family in different ways. She is empowered not only to talk more and ask questions about her departed family members, but also to develop boundaries and feel clarity about their interactions in a way that she did not before. She doesn't need to share with her entire family that she builds ancestor altars and talks to dead people in order to share the healing that she has derived from those practices. Healing also happens in families when relationships shift and one person models different behaviors, like not ignoring harm done, saying "no," and instituting personal limits within conversations. Teaching people how to treat you is a healing tool. Your ancestors and community also get to learn and heal from that, too.

Ancestral connection does not mean you have to be BFFs with your family members. It does not mean that you look past harm, abuse, and traumas that have been enacted on you by family members. It also does not mean that in order to be a good spiritualist, you have to get along with everybody . . . it is quite the opposite. Ancestral connection gives us the tools to really look and understand our families through a variety of lenses. It won't allow you to run away from the family stuff; instead it allows you face it directly, with new tools to navigate what you do with that information. Your ancestors learn from your boundaries, too. Sometimes they're like, "Dang, I didn't even know that was an option!" They may not have recommended a particular action until you showed them how it was done. In my experience, they bless you and protect you a little extra for that.

## CAN ANCESTORS BE HOMOPHOBIC?

As far as I know, no one in my immediate family is openly gay, queer, trans, or holds any of the gender- or sexuality-expansive identities. The only ancestor whom I know by name is my uncle David, who died before I was born during the AIDS crises of the late '80s and '90s. Stories of my ancestor David always warm my heart, as he is always described as beautiful and always dressing to the nines, and he won many modeling competitions in Baltimore. I imagine what my relationship to my own bisexuality could have been if I had a loving uncle around whom I could witness living in his truth. My ancestral relationship with Uncle David is strong, but it was not until I knew that I could acknowledge him that I felt less alone.

Unfortunately, my Uncle David had to be a trailblazer of queerness within my family. Although he was deeply loved and supported, there were parts of him that he had to hide, and I believe that he was not able to fully receive the love he deserved from our entire family, because of the harshness and stigma of AIDS. Understanding this complexity, I often think about my own identity and the desire to be fully supported by all members of my family. It's been a difficult journey that I will say has gotten much better but does have its setbacks. If I don't have any openly LGBTQ living family members and the one that I knew of didn't have an opportunity to have the support and acceptance that he deserved, what must my ancestors think of me? Are my ancestors homophobic?

I've had a very transformative albeit complicated relationship with my ancestors as it relates to my sexuality. I know that, at the beginning of my journey, I made a lot of assumptions about the homophobia of my ancestors because I was experiencing those phobias in my family. Although I am very fluid in who I date, I was very anxious when it came to my desire for women, and if my ancestors still loved me when I had girlfriends. How could they? Many of them were Christian or traditional people, with traditional family values and goals. I'm sure that they want me to be with a man and have children, to establish a legacy that they may be proud of, right? Not quite.

When I was a "baby witch" I believed that my ancestors did not like me and my girlfriend because of their homophobia. That is partially true ... they did not like me and my partner together. But it was not due to the homophobia as I thought: it was because they simply didn't like my partner. My assumptions led me to project my own internalized disdain onto myself around my sexuality, claiming it as theirs. An added layer to this complicated relationship is that my ancestors really want me to have children. Some of them were genuinely confused how that could happen in this sort of queer relationship. Fortunately I really want children too, and regardless of what person I end up with, children will always be a part of that narrative. This was something that I had to explain to them, because some of my ancestors did not realize that it would be possible for me to have kids! I told them to get with the times, and that coupling and family bearing had come a long way. They understood, and we kept it at that.

One of the reasons that I love ancestral relationships so much is because none of us know everything. We as humans do not know everything, and neither do our ancestors. It is a give-and-take relationship that involves a lot of communication, explaining, and getting our ancestors with the times. I had an ancestor from West Africa show up for me who absolutely did not understand my definitions of "queerness" or the choices I was making around partnership. So I explained my desires to her, and the opportunities around my choices of partners that she was not afforded. I came to realize that she understood what it meant to desire another woman but never to build a life or family with one. That piece was what was odd or confusing to her, not the attraction. She later revealed to me that she has felt the "queer" kind of love toward women, but her ability to choose to act on that was hardly an option or a thought worth exploring. In her mind, it was unbelievable to have freedom to choose that kind of connection, in such a way. Once we had this conversation and understood each other, a level of closeness developed between me and that ancestor. Our love deepened as we created a space to learn from each other, instead of assuming malicious intent. We created an opportunity to grow and listen.

Now, could an ancestor disprove of your sexuality or gender? Yes. Is that disapproval always rooted in a phobia? No. If your ancestors are concerned about children, let them know, as I did, that the gender of your partner is not a determining factor on your ability to have children. However, if you are not interested in children, that is something to share with your ancestors as well. Tell them that you understand that they may want to be reborn again for the legacy of their lineages, but they may have to find another descendant to do that through! Talk to them about your decisions: your whys, and their whys. You may be surprised at what may come forth from these kinds of conversations.

Remember that you do not have to engage with all your dead, especially if you feel that they don't value you or your identity. This is why I am always clear on saying, "I'm calling on my honorable ancestors who value and support who I am, and my personal destiny, fully." If you've got an ancestor who you think might be a hater, don't talk to them. Unless you are like me and always want to know why people think the way they do and whether it serves anyone in the lineage anymore. I try to remain open to all the possibilities and be sure I'm not projecting. Our people do know how to change, and it's an awe-inspiring moment when we can experience that change even in death.

You have ancestors of many different identities. Some were gay, some were disabled, some were gender nonconforming, some were sex workers, and some were around before there were even names for these kinds of things. Unfortunately, because of the injection of Abrahamic tradition, our ancestral relationships to what is "queer" have been perverted through colonialism. Sexuality also may not have been a "thing" for them (as it is for us in these current times) in whatever society they may have lived in. Elder Sobonfu Somé writes in her book *The Spirit of Intimacy* that, in Burkina Faso, members of indigenous Dagara communities who would be considered LGBTQ in our society were considered the "Gatekeepers." These individuals had specific roles, duties, and spiritual gifts that non-Gatekeepers were not able to access, unless they consulted with the Gatekeepers. Gatekeepers were respected for their magic in the village and valued for their ability to carry out certain rituals. This leads me to think that there were very real levels of separation and acceptance among groups—not so much rooted in homophobia, but in sharing space with others who had similar rituals, rites, initiations, and gifts. In some cases, when our indigenous ancestors show up, they very well may have been gatekeepers, but they also may have not been connected to the gatekeeper communities and thus do not have full understandings. It has been pivotal to me to remain curious about the kinds of identities that have existed, the language of the identities that we call ourselves, and the words we use to address our ancestors. They are not always the same.

## CAN MY ANCESTORS HEAL TRAUMA?

My relationship with my family is pretty standard. I have family members that I am closer to than others, there are family members I don't particularly care for but tolerate, and there are family members I absolutely adore. Like many people, I grew up in a house with divorced parents, an entire bonus family, and my fair share of childhood trauma. All these experiences inform what I've thought about my family and even how I relate to my ancestors. Like many children, I had some painful experiences in my childhood that were enacted through adults. The way that trauma works is sometimes we don't remember everything that happens to us, but we get triggered or have flashbacks of events that you don't even recall cognitively but *feel*. This was the case for me, except it was in my dreams. I would have regular disparaging dreams off and on for over ten years. Once I developed a relationship with my ancestors through divination, I was able to ask them if these visions meant anything. Repeatedly, through various self-divinations as well as consulting trusted practitioners of various religions including Hoodoo, Ifa, and even Palo . . . all my spirits confirmed that my dreams pointed to a deeper trauma that I experienced. I questioned why my ancestors chose to continuously show me these visions. I even felt like I hated them for not protecting me. What was the point of them reminding me of a trauma that I thought that I "forgot"? What was the reason for tormenting me in my dreams so I could relive such a sad time in my life, and what the hell was I supposed to do now? Well, you may be surprised that this opened up the floodgates of more experiences within my childhood—my traumas, my experiences, all the negative words that stayed with me, that I hadn't let go of. It reminded me that I had some deep healing to do, and I was being encouraged to address my issues with this person directly, and I did. I believe that I wouldn't have remembered this trauma without my ancestors showing it to me in my dreams. It showed me that we never actually forget. I never forgot. I could not go through my life not fully acknowledging this experience anymore. My psychic self recalled it, even if my conscious self did not, and my psychic body wanted to release that pain. My ancestors taught me that pushing things off and away is not healing. Trust that they probably know more about that than us, because how many older Black people do you know that are practicing vulnerability and honesty around emotions?

Only my ancestors could have worked with me for over a year to gain the courage to confront my childhood issues. They encouraged me to get back into therapy, supported me through immense grief, and even held my anger and resentment toward them. I bawled at my altar at almost every sitting, and I even decided to ignore my ancestors for a couple months because I was so angry over many things. Yet my confrontation with this person allowed me to lift a weight off of my shoulders that I did not know was there. I took my power back.

When I was having a conversation with a trusted friend and priestess within the Orisha community, she said that she believes therapy and practicing ancestral religion should go hand in hand. In many ways, she feels that it is even more important for people engaging with their ancestors more regularly to be enrolled in some kind of therapeutic practice that exists outside our regular rituals. She made an amazing point: people who choose to practice ancestral veneration are more likely to come into contact with their generational problems than the average person. In this work, we are actually being shown things, being told things via divination, and being required to show up and end some of the toxic cycles that have been passed down to us. We are in constant conversation and reverence with spirits who had difficult experiences and many of them are still trying to make sense of their lives and traumas. Hear me when I say that it is a lot. In addition to your elder, reader, or spiritual practitioner that you need support from, you will need help from someone to allow you to process all the new realizations and information that are coming up for you. Many will incorrectly state that, from a traditional standpoint, our ancestors turned to ritual and not therapy, and although that is true, we no longer live in indigenous times. Life, trauma, and pain are different. When our precolonial African ancestors venerated *their* ancestors, their problems were a lot different than our problems now. All societies throughout the ages have had their difficulties, but it could be argued that our current problems stem from not just one or two major issues, but myriad colonialisms, instabilities, acts of abuse, drug addictions, lack of natural resources (like clean water or air)—issues that simply may not have been prevalent in an indigenous society. Some of these problems are new, so we need new ways to address them that include our veneration rituals, and also someone who can support us in carrying all that comes with not only us, but our ancestors.

Some Orisha communities have a saying: "When you heal yourself, you are healing backward and forward seven generations." This means that when we allow ourselves to truly acknowledge our stories, ask ourselves (and maybe others) the important questions, address our shame and traumas, feel it, let it move through our bodies, and let it fall from our shoulders, we are also allowing our ancestors to release those same traumas. I am not the first person in my lineage to experience violence. In fact, many of my ancestors (and family members) have also been survivors of it. As you may remember, the original dream that connected me to my ancestors was the witnessing of a brutal rape of an ancestral mother, which eventually killed her. The experiences of our ancestors do not magically disappear when they die—they can often transform into familial habits and dynamics that are harmful to offspring and other community members. Some of these experiences travel through our DNA and end up affecting us in ways that no therapist can even reach, because they exist on a soul level.

Recurring problems that show up in bloodlines can also be less extreme. Attitudes as small as *my mother never complained about being overworked, so I don't complain about being overworked, and I expect that my children do not complain when I overwork them* are how ancestral habits are passed down, whether knowingly or unknowingly. When we begin to understand this dynamic, we can ask ourselves where this idea of overworking came from. Is it that my caregiver never needed rest, or was there something bigger than her, such as capitalism, that deeply impacted the ancestral and generational habits and traumas that my family has held onto? Asking these questions and then taking additional action can help heal those seven generations back that may not have had the opportunity to take a break, rest, or even ponder the idea. When you acknowledge your shit, know that it's probably not just yours, but that you have an ancestor who has been there, done that, and probably passed it down to you.

In addition to our generational traumas, we also can have generational joys! Our people did not just leave us full of bad habits, choices, and traumas, but an array of gifts, aptitudes, and blessings that benefit us, too. I may have had a family who never spoke about their problems, but boy are they amazing musicians, singers, dancers, and writers. The gifts of song and music are healing tools that I'm able to use to help address some of those generational traumas. Writing music, dancing, and musical theater have always been safe spaces for me to process and escape to a world full of happiness and joy that I've found through song. I'm grateful for my propensity for the arts and also recognize that many in my family were choir directors, hand dancers, and bandmates. Apparently I've got some relation to the pianist and composer Eubie Blake, so you see how the music loving runs deep. Remember that your ancestors left you with more than generational traumas. I love dancing in front of my altar or playing music that I think they would have liked. Saying, "Ancestors, dance with me, let's celebrate my promotion!" or asking, "Can my ancestors who were songwriters give me some inspiration for a new song?" are ways to bring the wisdom of the past into our lives.

## HOW CAN I TALK TO ANCESTORS WITHOUT KNOWING THEM?

As mentioned before, I know that some folks do not have deep connections to their blood families. It may seem difficult to seek connections with people that you've never met or aren't closely connected to, such as through adoption. But I think that people who are not closely connected to their blood families can still find ways to connect to them. Knowing names is not necessary, heirlooms are not necessary, nor are photos. You can still pray and simply say, "To my honorable ancestors who love me . . ." and begin your thanks and gratitude. You can also say, "Ancestors I don't know, but I'd like to know, please show me how we can grow closer."

If you're not interested in any of this, then don't do it. If you have people that you consider ancestors who are not related to you by blood, they still matter! Those of you who were adopted by others can still be impacted *deeply* by departed adoptive relatives and family members. I have a loved one who is quite a powerful dreamer, constantly dreaming of ancestors and spirits talking to her. She is also adopted, and these dreams are pretty much exclusively of her adoptive family. These dreams range from loving embraces and pride from the grandmother that raised her, to sometimes difficult dreams of her adoptive mother who did not care for her properly. This happens because these spirits are deeply intertwined in my friend's life, although they are not her blood relatives. In fact, some rituals needed to be completed so that her adoptive mother could rest easily and not keep showing up and giving my friend bad dreams.

Although blood ancestors often do come through to us, sometimes our access to them may be limited because of whatever experiences they had during human life. It's also important to note that spirits often "adopt us" and show up as our ancestors when they may not even be our relatives. I've said something like, "You have a woman who is showing up as an ancestor who says XYZ," and my client says, "I can't think of an ancestor who seems like that, but it sounds like my old neighbor who used to babysit me!" After further questioning, I realize that this babysitter has joined the ancestral court of my client. Maybe there is some relation between the babysitter and my client that they don't know. Everybody does seem like they're cousins in some way these days, but as far as we know this babysitter had no obvious familial relationship yet loves, cherishes, and protects this person as if she were her own, just as she did in life. Some people may consider the former babysitter a spirit guide, yet she was very much placed with the clients' ancestors and had quite a bit to say to her baby.

## HOW CAN I LEARN MORE ABOUT MY ANCESTORS?

One of the easiest ways that we can honor our ancestors and familial spirits is to share stories about them. If you can, ask people in your family about what Uncle So-and-so was like, or maybe ask your caregivers how they were raised. Hearing and understanding these stories can help create bonds and trigger forgotten memories within a family. Often, as people engage with ancestral spirituality, they want to talk to their families about whether anyone was a witch or practiced juju, but this may not be the best way to go about things! Simply ask general questions about the deceased's lives and personalities. Ask to hear stories about certain people that may interest you, and use those stories to then connect with your ancestors. They love when we remember them, and you can share some of those fond stories and memories with others as you learn them. This is a simple way to call on your ancestors' energy that is still very present. Hearing their names helps wake them up and get their attention.

If you don't have anyone to ask, you can always look up stories about people living in certain time frames, in certain cities, and among certain identities. For example, nobody who is living now knows any stories about any of my ancestors in Trinidad. On the surface, that history is completely lost, as my family members who were of that lineage all passed away when I was very young. However, I can look up the lives of Trinidadian people in the early 1900s. I can see what parts of Africa they may have descended from and what was happening politically, culturally, and socially in Trinidad during that time. I can also research why there was an influx of Caribbean people taken to Virginia in the early 1900s. Historical research can help me find connections to my ancestors, even if I do not have any names or personal stories to go off. I find that researching enslavement, migration, certain cities and towns, and even day-to-day living helps me piece together my own stories of my people. Remember the concept of the ancestral eye? That's a big piece of what guides my information seeking when I feel disconnected from my ancestors or don't have a lot of information to work from.

## DNA TESTS

Ancestral DNA tests have been another method that has helped me gain a more specific idea of my own ancestry and even connect with others who have similar DNA as mine through the sharing feature employed by certain companies. Of course there is a lot of conversation and concern around the use of DNA materials: is it safe, and is it worth the process of sharing such personal information? I think this is a decision that you have to make on your own. Do your research to choose a specific company and gain an understanding of their practices in order to safely move forward. There are tons of ancestry tests these days, and they all operate a little differently, so there is an array of choices available. That said, I've been able to garner a lot of great information from ancestral DNA tests that have connected me to cousins I would not have ever known otherwise. Even if you are not comfortable using your DNA for ancestral findings, some diviners use a method in divination to help you connect to your ancestors and ancestral homelands using the power of spirit—no spit required. Regardless of whether you choose a divinatory method, DNA methods, or both, your attempts are not in vain and your spirits will be sure that you get some clear answers over time.

Whether you are connected to specific tribal identities does not dictate the power or strength of your ancestry or lineage, however. If you are from Baltimore, and so was your family as far as you know, then start in Baltimore. There is medicine and ancestral connection for you in your hometown. A beautiful writer friend of mine, Hess Love, has shared her musings on this, which I believe are important to include here. Love

## CONNECTING WITH ANCESTORS YOU DIDN'T KNOW

Use this activity to imagine the faces of ancestors you may not have been connected with. This can be used by people who do not know any of their blood relatives or perhaps only a few and want to connect with other deceased human spirits of their lineages.

Do you know some ancestors personally? If not, that's okay! Think of your own face. Think about some of your features. Is your bottom lip very full? Are your legs hairy? Is your hair thicker in the middle, or are your eyelids naturally dark? Consider many of your features. Then imagine someone with similar features. Imagine a man with thick leg hair like yours, or a person who was short like you.

Now consider your personality. Are you typically anxious or calm? Do you have any special tics or ways that you communicate that make you unique? What are some of your quirks, or what random things make you so excited? Sit with some of those quirks and then go here:

Imagine someone else with a nose like yours or who used to blink excessively while speaking—whatever traits you'd like to focus on. Now think of that person's parents. What might they have looked like, or what kind of experience might they have had? How do you think they may have been raised, and what person could have informed their traits? Imagine their grandparents, and now their grandparents' parents. Go back as far as you can while still feeling connected and close. If you can only imagine back one or two generations, that's fine.

Now that you have some faces in your mind, including some that mirror your personality, say hello. Introduce yourself to these different faces. Say your name, and state your intention of giving faces to those you may not have met in the physical realm but who know you in spirit. Speak that you'd like to call on all your honorable ancestors and give them permission to make themselves known in your life through whatever method you are comfortable with (signs, dreams, smells, thoughts, etc.).

Continue this practice when you have quiet time and you want to connect deeper with your ancestors. This allows you to give faces and experiences to people that you may "feel" you made up, but who are really showing themselves to you in your mind's eye.

writes on ancestral connection: "The Great Migration included people moving from rural parts of the state to urban and suburban neighborhoods. Sometimes the connection you've been looking for is a two-hour drive away. Flying to Lagos or Montgomery ain't gon' help you when your people are from Cambridge, Maryland." This quote beautifully articulates the innate desire we may have to look for our ancestors outside our immediate locales; however, often what we are seeking is a lot closer to home than we think. Understanding the breadth and expansiveness of our ancestors is important, and acknowledging the many lands and waters they may have crossed can address some of our queries and connections, but remember that there is still an overflow of ancestral connection on the very land where you stand. The DNA tests will always be there to provide additional information if and when you'd like, but your indigenous tribal ancestors are equally as important as your granny from Chicago.

## HOW CAN I BE A BETTER DESCENDANT?

One of the most pivotal changes in how I venerate ancestors is my current focus on the importance of legacy. Often when people think of legacy, they consider the lives of their children or future children. Striving to be a good parent and possibly grandparent is a crucial aspect in forming a world that is safer, more loving, and desirable. I think the things we decide to do for and with our children are great examples of leaving a legacy, and prioritizing their care is such a huge responsibility that requires a lot of time, attention, and dedication. Although I am not a parent yet, my ancestors help me to formulate ideas that I believe will be necessary to share with my children, because they are sometimes still contending with choices that have negatively impacted my family. Children are beautiful legacies to leave as an extension of our spirits on earth, but having a child is not the only way to think about the power of legacy building.

When you engage with spirits and people who have passed on, they are constantly in conversation about the impact of their actions on others. It's not uncommon to get a few "I'm sorry for that" answers in divination, because after they pass our ancestors acquire a better understanding of their actions made while on earth. To be a part of and partially witness this transformation in death, we are confronted with the true meaning of our legacies. Simply put, we realize that we will one day need to be a good ancestor. This does not mean that we are constantly preparing for our death, but it is a realization that ultimately we will be in the position of the death process, which many say includes reconciling with the choices that we made in life. In the end, I imagine that you'll hope to have been a good steward of the land, of the spirit, and to others.

Our legacies often fuel our abilities to be revered spirits that are honored for our deeds and what we "left behind." What we leave behind could be the memories of always being the one to crack a joke, or the one who would offer to cook for everyone and invite people over. Maybe a piece of your legacy is always hooking up someone to get a new job or mentorship, or taking care of the family land. A piece of my legacy will be this book. Whatever legacy you carry, it is with hope that you can be a good ancestor, able to sit back and feel not just individually but communally accomplished, with a name that could never be forgotten because of the effect you had on the world around you. That doesn't have to be anything huge, like having six children or passing down fifteen acres of land—know that legacy is all-encompassing, and it's about adding value to the spaces that you're in. Understanding this, as well as the importance of legacy in Africana spiritual systems, gives me room to align my daily decision-making with something that I'm proud of. I'm regularly thinking, *how does this affect me today, how could this affect me in five years?* or *does participating in this thing make me feel proud of myself?* or *how do I want to be remembered?* Questions like these help us connect with our future selves, creating legacy blueprints to work from, so that our stories are ultimately both comprehensive and positive.

# BE A GOOD ANCESTOR ACTIVITY

This activity will help you think about your future goals and plans as they pertain to being a good ancestor. A good ancestor is one who lived a fulfilling life and made a palpable impact in the lives of the self and others. Think through some of these questions as a way to tap into your ancestral self!

What do you hope to be your legacy? What would you like to be remembered for?

If you were to look at a video mapping your entire life to this point, how would you feel about your decisions?

What is one thing that you're most proud of about yourself?

In what ways could you be better about planning for your legacies? How will you go about doing that?

What habit, tradition, or vice do you hope dies with you? Meaning, what must go when you go? Think small, like personal choices (ending the cycle of abuse in your family) or big (like helping address pollution in the world). How have you contributed to ending that thing, if at all? How might you?

# CHAPTER 13

# GOOD OLE RITUAL

I want to share with you tools and rituals, some you may know and some you may not have realized were available to help you address your needs. Ritual is the crux of life, and intentional ritual holds more power than you may expect. Seeking spiritual counsel is good and sometimes necessary, but there is nothing more accessible than the rituals you craft with your own body. This is by no means a comprehensive catalog of rituals, but you can add these simple ritualistic practices to your daily routine. As you delve into a specific spiritual tradition, you will learn additional rituals that are specific to your lineage, practice, and spiritual cosmology. Some of these are rituals that I've learned from various traditions during my years as a spiritualist, while others have been shared with me by ancestors who have given me permission to share them with you. These are easy ways to address the everyday concerns we may have and enjoy a more abundant and protected life.

As I've mentioned before, there is a ritual for everything! Our ancestors are wonderful because they've been able to pass down many rituals so that we can have the best experiences on earth. Unpopular opinion here, but old wives' tales and superstitions are simply rituals for our benefit. Although they seem like silly happenings that have no rhyme or reason, they are often rooted in a belief system and have undergone a lot of "personal experiments" with negative or positive effects that have led to the persistence of the ritual throughout generations. There is a reason that my grandma says that on New Year's Day, a man must walk through your door *first* with money in his pocket to bring about prosperity for the year. It sounds silly, and perhaps unnecessary because "Why a man?" and "Why he gotta come in my house?" but clearly this ritual has worked for the people around her and generations before her (she got this from her mother). I asked my very Christian grandmother why she has my father do this every year, and she said, "I don't know why, but we always did it growing up and it worked for my mother. As long as you believe it'll work, it will. And as long as you have Jesus." Although I've regularly questioned the relevance of the Jesus part, this ritual may be a nod to the spirit of the crossroads, which can exercise significant control over our access to financial stability. Walking through a threshold with money on the first day of the New Year may be a form of acknowledging the crossing into a new energetic year, and a money offering to the spirits who live at the threshold between the living and the dead. This may signal to the crossroads spirit that we'd like to have a financially abundant year! Please be clear: I don't know if that's the reason—I could have just made all that up (sounded damn good though, that's GOT to be it). But the message is to be mindful of not writing off seemingly silly rituals because they don't make sense to us. Although every tale is not relevant to every single person, and some are regional and family specific, if there are ones that stand out to you, it may be something worth looking into! Rituals, as a new person engaging in them, may not make sense, but that could be because we aren't a culture that is immersed in intentional ancestral rituals. The more you learn about the variety of rituals and their outcomes, the less nonsensical they become. Believe that it all has meaning, whether obvious or not. Know, too, that we aren't to know or understand the specifics of every single ritual. Some things we get to learn in time, and some things we just do while having faith in our ancestors. Trust me, not knowing some things is a blessing.

The spiritual realm is said to mirror our experiences in the physical realm. So, if we have a pesky person bothering us at work, there may also be a spirit in the spirit realm being a bother, and thus ritual can help set the spirit (and the person) straight. When that spirit is set straight on the spirit plane, it can then mellow out our experience on earth. That is why ritual is so important. However, it is important that we address both the spiritual and the physical to have the most effective outcome. Ritual on its own is not the only method to address your concerns. There is a great misconception that one can sacrifice a rooster and all your issues will be abolished, but that is not the case. Baking your ancestral mothers a cake will not heal you of all your worries and doubts. It may sweeten your life and give you the energetic tools to manipulate your current situation, but if you receive blessings and are not able to enjoy them because you sabotage all that is good, for example, your offering has gone to waste. Making a change in your life requires ritual, sacrifice, time, commitment, dedication to your goals, support, self-love, and energetic support. And keep in mind that it's also not always your season. Perhaps you've been going through a rough patch, and sometimes it's simply a rough patch, no more and no less. As my Olúwo has said to me, "We would not know sweetness if we did not know bitter. Sometimes shit just sucks and the ritual is to try your best and wait it out." What do the Christians say? "Trouble don't last always"—they got that part right.

Give your rituals time to work. Sometimes after receiving instructions from a reading, we go and do what our ancestors told us to do, yet we still feel conflicted or out of whack. Make sure that you're letting the juju get to you! Things do not happen overnight, and these are not microwave traditions. There are of course ways to speed up your manifestations, but overall, let the work work. Most importantly, trust yourself and your ancestors. There is no reason you should be appeasing spirits that you don't even trust will help you. Belief is such a big part of your spiritual connections, rituals, and manifestations. You must trust that things *can* change for you. If you're struggling with trusting your ancestors, ask them to teach you how to trust. Tell them that you're struggling, and that you need extra support to know that all is working out for you. Tell them that you're nervous, scared, and struggling. Speak to your ancestors not only about your concerns about money and love; include your anxieties, worries, and doubts.

## INTRODUCTORY RITUALS

The following are some basic rituals to help center your mind and body— no extras needed. Rituals involving grounding and breath can be simple ritual add-ons with very big results.

### BREATHE, CHILE.

I know it's corny, I know everybody says it, and I know it is often suggested at times we don't want to hear it, but—we have to breathe. This is why colds can be so miserable to us, because we are struggling to pull air into our lungs when all we want to do is breathe clearly. Breath is sacred, and breath is the source of life, and not just in a metaphorical esoteric way, but in the very literal way. You must breathe to live. Practice this simple breathing exercise as a way to get in touch with your breath and help your brain relax.

Firmly plant your feet on the floor, whether you are standing or sitting. Uncross your legs, arms, and unclench any parts of your body that feel stiff (if you're like me, unclench that jaw and let your tongue relax in the bottom of your mouth). Close your eyes or find a soft gaze in a corner of a room, on focus on something comforting, yourself, or even the floor.

Inhale through your nose slowly and intentionally, hold for three seconds, and exhale through your mouth, audibly if you can. You should notice your tummy expand while you do this breathing exercise. The air should flow deep into your body and be expelled through your mouth. As much as you can only focus on the process of inhaling and exhaling, let your breath be the center of your thoughts. Let the inhale and exhale be your primary focus in this moment, for all the other thoughts will be there when we are finished. Some people recommend doing this three times, some people will say five, and I say do it as many times as you need to.

## GROUNDING

Although breathwork is a form of grounding, we can also connect to nature and plant matter for similar purposes. Being barefoot in grass or dirt or putting our hands on the land can help us gain a lot of clarity. Try practicing the breathing exercise above while standing in the grass, or simply stand barefoot on your floor while you do it.

Plants help bring grounding energy into the home if you're not easily able to access nature. Repotting plants, or even resting your hands in the soil, can provide a powerful medicine. If you're trying to access clarity, ask the flourishing plant a question, and then press your hands firmly into the dirt. You can also gather items from outdoors like small sticks, rocks, dirt, and plants, then keep them in a small pouch that you carry with you for grounding!

## NATURAL RITUALS

Contrary to popular belief, anyone *can* access the Orishas, because we all live in the natural world and Orishas are personified deities of the natural elements. To be clear, though, unless you have the proper tools and initiatory rites, it is not advisable to summon them based on your own rituals. There are specific ways that priests and practitioners access Orishas, because they have learned how to do so at their respective sacred locations (such as rivers, marketplaces, or during storms) or at their designated shrines.

We are not all able to summon the Orishas because it takes a certain level of knowledge; however, we are all able to commune with the natural entities as members of this world. For example, you may want to bring more love, success, compassion, and care to your life. Or perhaps you may feel like you're going through a period where you're feeling misunderstood and need closeness and care. Based on the Yoruba pantheon, you may want to visit the water deity Oshun in order to access some of these qualities. Oshun is often seen as a protective mother. She defends and protects her children fiercely and also enjoys giving them some of the most beautiful things that life has to offer. But it's important to note that water deities go by many names depending on the cultural lineage and belief system of the particular region in which they originate. Mami Wata, Ọṣun, Yemọja, mermaids, Sobek, Agwé, Ogbuide, Ma Lago, and hundreds—perhaps thousands—of other names exist to acknowledge the divine mysteries of the waters. Regardless of the name, water is a spirit and ancestor in itself that you can access. It does not need to go by the name Oshun to work for you.

Recently I spoke with my friend Alafia, who is a priestess of the river deity Oshun in the traditional Yoruba pantheon. I asked her if sharing a ritual that was acceptable for a layperson to connect with Oshun would be appropriate in this book, because I wondered how people who are not in the tradition may leave offerings to Oshun and connect with her. Instead of providing a ritual to do this, she said that often she goes to the river to connect with the water as its own entity separate from her relationship with Oshun. She also says that she likes to go to the water to connect with her own ancestors and does not always leave fancy offerings. "When things are in a heightened state," she says, "I offer my tears back to the water."

You see, water, land, tree, dirt, fire, and every other energy within nature—they are all spirits within themselves. The many names for these spirits differ among regions, but what does not change is the element itself. Connect with water as water, connect with land as land, connect with air as air. The natural elements are spirits. If you desire to personify them, that is your prerogative, but it is important to research and possibly even talk to an elder in that tradition for more information on how to get to know that personified deity (as they may have taboos or special things that they like). But know that you can go to the water without knowing its "name" and still talk to it, pray to it, and leave even just your tears as offering.

## CONNECTING WITH WATER

Water is a beautiful element that provides comfort, love, and protection. We know that it nourishes, cleanses, and purifies, but it also drowns. Water is the life source for all living things, as we would not exist without it. Not only does water nourish us, but it often provides us with beautiful and vast scenery. People pay a lot of money for boats so they can sit on the water, they embark on road trips to the beach to watch and frolic in water, and they even take their entire family to water parks to make fun memories. We use water for everything from cooking to cleaning. A nice hot bath or a shower can sometimes make a world of a difference in our moods. Water is life!

Conversely, although water brings us life, joy, and beauty, we are also familiar with its destructive nature. Hurricanes and torrential rains can ruin homes and communities. Water can flood an entire city within a few days and sometimes hours, and drowning may be one of the most horrific ways to die. Water has the ability to carry the duality of existence within its ever-flowing body, and because our ancient ancestors knew this, they encouraged being in right relationship with water. Our Hoodoo ancestors knew that water rituals can make someone spiritually clean and new. Old photos of Black folks walking down to the river to baptize someone depict an event that existed not only because the participants desired to give their life to Christ. Water also represented a new day, and water ritual was familiar to enslaved Africans and their descendants in the southern United States.

Water is an ancient spirit with a lot of wisdom that we should connect with as much as we can. If you can get down to a local river, stream, or beach I would encourage doing that. Some offerings for the water could be prayers, fruits, honey, wine, flowers, coconuts, and sometimes jewelry. Regardless of the offering, be sure that it is biodegradable so that you are not adding to the pollution of our precious resource. Remove bottles, plastic coverings, and other materials that are not necessary from what you leave. Beach cleanups or simply gathering trash while visiting water sources are other great offerings to provide to the water spirits. In my experience, the spirit of water enjoys being beautiful, and any action that supports this beauty is an offering that is always accepted. If you decide to go to the water, speak to it. Introduce yourself, state your claims, and give your offerings. Speak to the water with reverence, and tell her what you need. Cry, wail, and, if the water is clean enough, feel free to pray and sprinkle some of it on the back of your neck, hands, and feet as a blessing. As long as you are sincere, the water will hear you, because she hears everything. Ask for what you desire, give your offerings, and enjoy your time with her.

I am a water baby through and through as a triple Cancer in tropical astrology, and a child of Ọṣun. Water makes me feel alive, and with it I believe I can accomplish anything. I do know, however, that visiting lakes, oceans, or beaches is not accessible to everyone. Some of us live in places where there is hardly access to clean water, let alone a nice beach. If this is the case, there are many ways that you can connect with water and still reap its benefits.

1. A bath or shower. While you are bathing, speak to the water. Pray and say blessings over yourself and your life. Give thanks to the water for cleansing you and allow it to clear you of any stress or trauma you may be carrying. I like to imagine that a bunch of spiritual gunk is going down the drain as I'm showering, and I pray that the water cleans me not only physically, but spiritually and emotionally as well.

2. A foot bath. A foot bath is great because you can soak your feet and enjoy a peaceful moment to yourself. Although the water is not active (or moving, as in a shower), a foot bath is a good moment to take some time and connect with water as a source of calmness. A dash of Epsom or table salt in a foot basin works great, because salt is also used in Hoodoo as a cleanser. Salt can pull toxins and spiritual mess out of our bodies, so a salt and water combo is great for not only relaxation but for spiritual cleansing, too.

3. Spiritual baths. Spiritual baths are created with various materials, usually herbs and plant matter, that are compiled into a mixture and poured over the body for blessings. There are spiritual baths for protection, baths for cleansing,

baths for mental health, and even baths to get over a lover! There is a bath that can be made for everything because water can address all issues, and there is an herb that works for everything. Combining the power of herbal medicine with the power of water creates an extremely potent mixture that can aid our bodies, minds, and spirits. Spiritual baths are an active way to remain "spiritually clean" and better our spiritual hygiene. And you do not have to have a bathtub to take a spiritual bath! Many can simply be poured over the body after you have done your normal shower routine.

## SPIRITUAL HYGIENE

Spiritual hygiene is of utmost importance to engaging in ritual in general. Spiritual hygiene rituals are some of my favorite rituals that our ancestors have passed down, as they can often facilitate our desired outcomes when we "manifest." I know there are many people who constantly perform rituals to get things, like money rituals and I-want-a-boo rituals, and general manifestation works in order to bring in the good stuff. All this is perfectly fine, but sometimes people find themselves confused because their money rituals aren't working or they can't manifest their desires. Oftentimes this person is trying to attract the good stuff, but it's hard for the money spells to work because there is so much spiritual gunk on them that there is no room for the money or blessings to come forth. It can be hard to see or embrace the good things when there is such a spiritual heaviness.

Just as our bodies must be regularly cleaned from dirt or grime, so do our spirits. Energy is real, and in a spiritually congested world, it's easy to pick up on the emotions, feelings, and thoughts of others. Spiritual pestilence is just as prevalent as everyday dirt, and it must be addressed in order to maintain your protection and everyday balance. In many ways, this kind of hygiene can look like spiritual bathing, cleansing soaps, smoke cleanses, nature cleanses, or more. As long as you are engaging in a practice that seeks to cleanse you spiritually, you are engaging in a spiritual hygiene practice.

There is no strict number of times that you must spiritually cleanse yourself. Some people take spiritual baths every day, while some people may take them once a week or even once a month. Certain people need baths more than others, and it all depends on your personal routines, and what your spirit and body need. People who live in busy or congested cities sometimes need to cleanse themselves more often than someone who lives in a small rural town. People who identify as empaths, as well as professional spiritual practitioners, often need a consistent hygiene practice to avoid taking on the energies of people they may be reading or working with. Sometimes a lack of spiritual hygiene is the reason why we feel stressed, sad, or even upset. It's possible to take on other people's feelings and emotions without even realizing it! Spiritual cleansing helps us to make sure that our emotions are our own and that our spiritual boundaries are strong.

I'm someone who takes spiritual baths pretty regularly. Of course, there will always be earthly issues and problems, but engaging in this work has made me realize my personal "bullshit threshold," which is the normal amount of bullshit that you can endure in your day-to-day life. Flat tires, crying babies, and overdue credit card bills are normal issues that may present themselves in your life, but if you have these issues weekly on top of losing your wallet, getting a stomach virus, breaking your finger, and having your car stolen . . . you may want to see what's going on from a spiritual standpoint. Those moments when you feel like you absolutely cannot catch a break may mean that there is an underlying issue to be addressed spiritually.

## WHITE BATHS

White baths are one of the most powerful baths that you can take because of their ability to address our mental health concerns and help bring peace to our heads. I learned about white baths in the context of Lucumí, a sect of the Ifa Orisha tradition that uses a lot of coconuts and the color white within the practice. Coconuts are understood as healing tools, and the meat and coconut milk inside the coconut can help address mental health issues and concerns of the mind, including bad dreams and thoughts. White represents purity and is refreshing, and a white bath like this one can help with cleansing our Ori (elevated spiritual selves) by bringing peace to our heads.

Making a white bath is fairly easy, and there are various ways to do it. A standard white bath simply needs cool water and milk, in my opinion, but there are other materials that can help amplify your bath. Here's one for you to try:

**WHAT YOU WILL NEED**:
>A bowl
>Coconut, goat, or cow milk
>Cool water
>Florida Water or your favorite feel-good cologne
>White flower petals
>Cascarilla/Efun (ground eggshells)

Take your bowl and fill half of it with milk, then the other half with water. Add a pinch of the other materials if you have them. Mix gently, and pray into your bowl as you do so. Ask the bath to assist in uplifting your head, and confirm that you are allowing it to bring peace in your life. This is a sample prayer that you may use as you make your white bath:

> May this bath be blessed with the medicine needed to bring me inner peace, healing, and a balanced head. May I know peace through the powers of this bath and with the guidance of my Ori. Allow the milk to bring a clear head, that I may move forward in this world in better spirits and self-understanding. My head is blessed; may it bring me unexpected blessings. Do not let my mind confuse or trick me. Let this bath cleanse me from the unknown and known pains that I carry in my mind. May my mind be kind to me and align with my highest and most powerful destiny. Ase.

Do your normal bath or shower routine and, when you've finished, pray over the bath again if you'd like and then put the mixture over your head. Yes, baby, your hair is going to get wet, because it is crucial that this bath touches your *scalp*. I know this may not be the ideal bath for our hair and you may be internally screaming, but people have managed to get very creative around how to address the scalp only as much as possible. Feel free to do what you need, but this bath needs to touch your head, because that is what it is addressing.

Use this bath for as many days as you need. Typically I will take this bath in increments of odd numbers like three, five, or nine days. My only recommendation is to do it for as long as you need to and until you start to feel relief. Come back to this bath at a later date whenever you need it. In my opinion, you can never take too many white baths!

## GET OVER THEM BATH

Black walnut baths are wonderful baths to take to cut and clear ties to previous lovers and old friends. Perhaps you still feel a strong connection to someone that you no longer want to be connected to, and black walnut baths can help spiritually sever these ties so we can move on!

**WHAT YOU WILL NEED:**

Black walnuts

Water to boil

Add nine whole black walnuts (or a cup of ground black walnuts) to a pot over water. Bring the water to a boil. Let the walnuts boil for about thirty minutes until the water is completely black. Add more water if necessary. Pray into the mixture to remove and cut ties from the person you want to be released from. Let the water cool when complete. You may strain or remove the walnuts from the water if you'd like. After your regular shower or bath, pour the mixture over your body while praying to get over this previous person or thing. Repeat this ritual as necessary for three, five, or nine days—until you feel the connection being lessened.

## BASIC CLEANSING BATH

Use this bath as an easily accessible bath used to cleanse you of unnecessary energies that may be dragging you down.

**WHAT YOU WILL NEED:**

A bowl

Salt

Lemon or lime

Fresh mint

Mix the lemon or lime juice, mint, and salt in a bowl of cool water. While you're mixing, pray that these ingredients are activated to bring you spiritual cleanliness. Pray that this bath addresses any spiritual gunk that may be on you, and for this bath to refresh your aura and energy. After your normal shower or bath, pour this mixture over your body while praying for your cleansing. This is a bath you can do regularly to maintain spiritual hygiene.

## FRUIT CLEANSING RITUAL

This cleansing ritual does not use water! Use some old or unwanted fruit as a way to remove negative and unwanted energies from your sphere. You can also use a bunch of flowers or other natural living materials.

### WHAT YOU WILL NEED:

> A fruit of your choice (try a hefty fruit like an apple, banana, mango, or orange)

Rub the fruit over your entire body, starting from your crown and working your way down to your feet. Pay extra attention to your head, the back of your neck, your stomach, and your feet. Imagine the energy you want to release being transferred to the fruit while you chant the following prayer, or use words of your own:

> To my beloved ancestors, those who guard, protect, and open the way to all my blessings, I call you now. I ask for your assistance as I willfully remove all toxins, nasty energy, evil eye, bad juju, and general spiritual filth that may have covered me without my knowing. May my spirit be open to releasing all that no longer serves me onto this piece of fruit, as I dispose of it, never to be in contact with its energy again. Ase.

Once you're finished, dispose of the fruit in the trash can or at the crossroads! It is preferable to take the trash out afterward.

## PROTECTION RITUALS

Use these simple rituals to increase the protection rituals around yourself or your home:

- **Talk to your doors before leaving your home.** Ask for protection for everyone and everything inside and pray that nothing that doesn't belong is welcomed inside.
- **Carry protective amulets.** Amulets are objects that carry a specific intention or purpose. Protection is such an important aspect of any spiritual practice and can help keep ourselves safe. Choose an item that you'd like to be a protection amulet. This could be a cross that you like, a silver ring you love, or a High John root. Whatever you decide, cleanse the item with Florida Water, incense, or liquor. Place this item on your altar for nine days, asking that your ancestors infuse the energy of ancestral safety and protection onto your item. After the nine days, carry this item with you or place it in your car, home, or wherever you'd like to strengthen your protections. Once a month, you can put the item back on your altar for a "recharge," or simply keep it on your altar daily when it's not in use.

## PROSPERITY RITUALS

Prosperity is a necessity and desire for most of us! Who doesn't want a little extra money? I felt it was important to add a prosperity work in this book. This is one that my ancestors shared with me to share with others.

## PROSPERITY SPRAY

This easy-to-make spray is a great way to manifest your desires and prosperity into your life. Spray on yourself, in your rooms, or on items (like a wallet, purse, or cards) to assist in manifesting your wishes. If you skip the alcohol, this could also be used as a prosperity bath!

**WHAT YOU WILL NEED:**

1 teaspoon honey

Pinch of cinnamon

Pinch of rosemary

Bowl full of a mixture of half water and half preservative (such as alcohol that is at least 120 proof)

(Note: Use your own discretion with these amounts and follow your spirit!)

**WHAT TO DO:**

Place your honey, cinnamon, and rosemary in a bowl of water and alcohol preservative. Use this prayer as you combine the mixture or say your own words:

> To my beloved ancestors and spirits who guide me and bring me closer to my blessings and good manifestations, I call you. My ancestors who are well versed in joy, blessings, gifts, love, money, and prosperity in all its forms, come. May the ingredients of this working separately and collectively bring to me my heart's desires as aligned with my highest good. May the water bring me pure blessings. May the honey bring me a sweet life. May the cinnamon bring easeful finances, and the rosemary protect me from all that may be blocking my prosperity. Let this work speak for itself. May prosperity always be my portion. Ase.

Finally, pour your mixture into a spray bottle and spray away! Keep your spray refrigerated for longer preservation.

## ANCESTOR MONEY WORKING

Place money on your ancestor altar! I recommend that the bill be $5 or more, but if you only have a dollar or less, that will suffice. As you put the money on your altar, ask that your ancestors "flip" the amount to a number greater. I also like to give regular offerings of money to pay off any ancestral debts that may exist, and boost the flow of my own money. I do not spend the bills I place on the altar. Once it's on the altar, it's my ancestors' unless they tell me otherwise. If that's the case, it usually will go to a charity or someone on the street who needs it. This is a money work in itself. Some people do use fake "ancestor money" and even burn it on or near their ancestor altar as an offering. These bills are sold at various shops and you can use them if you like; however, my ancestors never cared much for fake tender.

## ANCESTRAL WRITING RITUAL

This ritual is a perfect one to take to your ancestor altar if you're trying to gain more information or clarity from them.

This ritual is simple and requires only a pen and a journal that you use specifically for your ancestral communication. Once your altar is set, you will sit in front of your altar. Be sure to light your candle, greet your ancestors, and pour your libation to honor their spirit, as you would normally. You may also burn incense if you have it. Next you'll pick a topic and set an intention that your ancestors will guide your writing. Then you'll write whatever is coming to mind. Simply allow yourself to journal until you're through. This is a great practice for writers or people who would like to incorporate journaling into their daily practices. I've been able to get a lot of clarity, insight, and even answers to my questions simply through writing with my ancestors and asking them to guide my words. Repeat this practice regularly—it can even be a form of divination through channeling your ancestors in written word.

## COLOR INCORPORATIONS

Colors are very important, especially for our clothing, our homes, and any other items we intentionally surround ourselves with. Like everything, colors carry specific kinds of energies that can be helpful or harmful to us depending on our intention and desired outcomes. Sometimes wearing black can cause more harm to us than good, or maybe we need to wear blue on a certain day. Here are some color meanings that have been helpful to me on my journey.

- *White:* In many African and diasporic traditions, you will often see people wearing a lot of white for ceremonial purposes. In many West African religions, white is a powerful color, as it is brings clarity, peace, protection, and calming. Usually a person in full white signifies some kind of rebirth, cleansing, or celebration! If you've been feeling a little "off" lately, it may be time to pull your whites out to bring some additional coolness to you. Wearing white is good when you need a refresh, some peaceful energy, or need to be calm in certain situations. I personally can never go wrong with an all-white 'fit, but pay attention to how you feel in certain colors.
- *Black:* Black is not a color that is commonly worn in Orisha-based practices, but I do see more black in Hoodoo spaces as well as Voodoo traditions mixed with other colors to portray certain loa or other spirits whose colors include black. Black is an absorbing color, representing the darkness, depth, the unseen world, death, and the things that

are hidden. Sometimes as we are trying to get deep into the metaphorical shadows (which can often be protective), black can be a shield or allow us to get to move beyond the surface.

- *Red:* Red is a color that is hot! Like fire, red can bring out our fiery, passionate, sexual, and energetic sides. Reds can also bring about the energy of protection and standing up for ourselves. I recall a reading that I had many years ago with a client who was extremely shy and believed that she couldn't stand up to a colleague who was walking all over her. Her ancestors instructed her to put on a red shirt and have a conversation with this person ASAP and speak her truth. Red can give us the extra power that we need to control our environments. Spicy red peppers on the tongue can also be a way to "heat" your intentions, prayers, and manifestations to amplify them, but be cautious! If you're naturally a hothead or feel that you don't need any extra help being spicy, be mindful of how you incorporate the reds into your life.

- *Yellow:* Yellow is a bright and sunny color usually associated with happiness and joy. Yellow prayer candles are often used to draw in money because of yellow's association to gold and wealth.

- *Green:* Green is, of course, the color of money, particularly in the United States. But it has broader associations with wealth, grounding, heart healing, and our connection to nature. Wear it when you want to bring abundance into your life.

- *Blue:* When you're looking to open the channels of good communication, wear blue. It also promotes peace and calmness, so it's good for days when you're feeling stressed and overwhelmed.

- *Purple:* When we think of purple, we think of nobility and wealth. Wear it when you're seeking an elevated status in society, a positive change in your life, or otherwise want to feel regal and powerful.

- *Brown:* If you're facing a court case, wear brown—it will give you luck. It's also a grounding energy and emphasizes our earthly connection.

## CHOOSING A PRACTICE

As you continue to build relationships with your ancestors with consistent communication, listening, and perhaps regular divination, you may feel yourself being called to specific spiritual or religious practices. As a Black American, you may want to delve deeper into Hoodoo, as this practice may have been beneficial to your ancestors. You also may seek to learn about other traditions like Nigerian Yoruba or Ghanaian Akan traditions and delve more into those deities, pantheons, and belief systems. This is normal! Many humans are looking for spiritual practices and frameworks that allow them to better make sense of their lives and the world around them. Many Africana-based spiritual practices can help us feel more connected and provide us with clear rituals to address any and all life concerns. Follow your intuitive self and the nudges from your ancestors to choose what feels right for you.

Some people are also perfectly fine not engaging in a formal religious practice, and solely center their ancestors for encouragement, guidance, and ritual. It is up to you. Study them all if you'd like, and learn the similarities and differences between various religious systems. Understand that you probably have ancestors who presented themselves through cross-cultural identities, so you may not be guided to only one. Your journey is yours; however, be sure that you are not rushing into any practices or initiations before you do proper research and communicate with other people who are a part of that practice. Ancestral connection is important for this reason. There is a level of curiosity and glamour that attracts us to the mystery of Africana and indigenous medicine systems. It can be easy to thrust yourself headfirst into a religion without the proper understanding or even building a relationship to your own spirits. Your ancestors will guide you through the process, if it is necessary for you. Just know that the ancestors come first and foremost in most if not all indigenous and indigenous-rooted healing systems. There is nothing that happens in your life that doesn't cross them first. You have a direct connection to source through them. You are the direct contact to the gift of your lineage through your ancestors. Nobody in any practice should be telling you that you need them in order to connect with your own ancestors. This is why I say to be sure that your foundation is strong before you start introducing new deities into your life. I love my deities and work with them regularly, but I make sure that home is taken care of, too. Home is your ancestors.

# CHAPTER 14

# GRIEF, DEATH, AND DYING

Grief is a natural human experience and one that can be among the most painful. Whether we are grieving the loss of a relationship, a person who has passed, or the end of an experience, grief has a funny way of making itself known. It can haunt us or blindside us as we try to find meaning while we long for something to which we no longer have access. We grieve lives that we could have lived, people we could have loved, and things we could have done. On some days grief feels far away, like a distant relative, and on other days it's the fly that just won't leave us alone, buzzing and irritating us without regard.

Grieving a loved one is a special kind of pain that ancestral connection has helped me address in very clear ways. On days that the grief feels too heavy, I go to my ancestor altar, whether inside or out in nature, and I let it out. I talk directly to what it is that I am grieving. In the most recent case, I speak clearly to my grandma. I light a candle and ask my ancestors to soothe me in my sad moments. I ask that they don't forget me, and that they speak to me in ways that are clear so I can understand. I pray for their continued elevation in the spiritual realm, and ask them to look upon me with favor and compassion as I learn to grow in love with them from another realm.

## GRIEF RITUALS

There are many grief rituals extending across multiple faith traditions that support me in difficult moments. Remember that in the midst of your grief you don't and shouldn't have to hold it alone. Here are some wonderful rituals that worked for me:

## CONNECTING WITH NATURE

This includes going on walks, visiting the river or an ocean, sitting in the park, or taking care of plants, as activities that involve nature always support me in handling grief. Nature, one of our oldest ancestors, is always there to listen and hold us, as it has since the beginning of time.

## ANCESTRAL ELEVATION

Sometimes our grief is more than our own. Many of our ancestors have lived traumatic lives and may still be grieving their experiences. Those of us who are connected to those ancestors may carry grief that was passed on to us. Grief can be a collective experience that we share with spirits, and sometimes addressing it is addressing ancestral grief as well. One way to do this is through an ancestral elevation ritual.

This ritual can take many days, but I will share a variation that I learned early in my journey as a Hoodoo. For nine days, you must pray fervently for the healing of your ancestors and ancestral lineage. Pray that they release their human woes and problems that keep them from embracing their elevation into ancestorship. Light a candle each day to honor ancestors who may be struggling or grieving. On day one, take a candle and a glass of cool water to the lowest point in your home (such as on the floor of your home apartment or a basement). Light the candle and pray for the healing and elevation of your ancestors, then repeat this step every day until the ninth day. You can replace the water if it starts to look foggy. On each day, lift the candle slightly higher. So, on day one, your candle and water will be on the floor, and on day two you may light your candle and place it and the water in a slightly higher place (like on top of a book). On day three, you may move both to a coffee table, on day four, you might place these tools on top of two books on the coffee table, and so on until you reach the ninth day, when your offerings will be at the highest point, you do your final prayer, and then you dispose of your candle and spiritual water. Some people may choose to add other offerings like candies, honey, and other sweet things to assist in the ancestral elevation. This ritual can be done repeatedly for specific ancestors or for your ancestors as a group who may need the additional support.

## FIRE RITUAL

If there is a specific experience that is bringing you grief that you'd like to remove from your sphere, a clearing ritual may be just what the juju doctor orders. On a piece of paper, right down the person, situation, or experience that you are trying to clear away. From the top of your head to the bottom of your feet, use the paper to cleanse the grief. Imagine the grief is like little pieces of metal on your body, and the paper with your written grievances is a powerful magnet pulling the issues from you. When you feel you are finished, fold the paper *away from you* repeatedly until it is as small as it can be. In a fire pit, cauldron, or another safe location, cast the small piece of paper into the fire. This is a wonderful ritual to do during the waning moon.

## CLEANSING

A huge aspect of addressing grief and spiritual mess is hygiene! As we've discussed prior, spiritual filth can aid in our feelings of sadness and even depression. Spiritual baths can aid in washing some of the grief away, not that you may no longer feel it but so that it's not continuously piling up on you to the point that you cannot manage it.

## PLANT MEDICINE

Try using these herbs for feelings of grief. They're best incorporated into spiritual baths and rituals and are not necessarily for consumption:

Lavender (induces calm)

Rose (increases love and positive relationships)

Marjoram (provides protection from sad events)

Motherwort (strength, protection)

Hyssop (removes jinxes)

Mint (encourages a strong sense of self)

## GRIEF IS JUST LOVE WITH NOWHERE TO GO

Remember that grief, like anything, is spirit. It has a life and a body of its own. It communicates in its grief language and tells us what it wants. We can make enemies with this spirit or we can listen to it. We can try to cuddle up next to it, or shun it away. As a spirit, it can be manipulated and even work for us. We can channel that grief into something powerful, as it is a malleable deity, always available and ready for us to acknowledge its presence. Grief can be a little selfish, but she never comes without a message that we may need; those messages tend to come later, when we've calmed down. Grief is a wise life force that doesn't care what class, race, or gender you are. She's a bad muhfucka' and should be respected as such.

One of the most important aspects and rituals of grief is that you must allow yourself to feel it. Grief, because it is uncomfortable, is often a feeling that we want to bypass or wish away. It can be easy to numb and ignore it—it ain't never been fun, and I wouldn't wish it on my worst enemy. However, feeling is the first aspect of any ritual, especially when it comes to grief. In this society, we are often pressured, directly or indirectly, to detach ourselves from our feelings, suppressing our emotions and hiding our grief in plain sight. To be well, we have to know what's going on with our minds and bodies. We need to feel, because we are human. A common quote I often think about is from the author Jamie Anderson: "Grief is just love with no place to go." Particularly when dealing with the grief of losing a loved one, I find this quote particularly helpful. The powerful part around ritual and being immersed in spiritual practice is that we can create containers where this orphaned love can go: in altars, our plants, our children, or our friends. When grief creeps up without invitation, we can invite it to sit with us at the altar, and we can talk to that person we miss so much. If we are grieving an aspect of our lives, we can ask our ancestors to show us gentleness and compassion, while also giving us new memories and experiences that will spark joy in our hearts. When we do this work, we will always have a place for that love and grief to go—in fact, we *have* to if we want to live full lives and become good ancestors ourselves. We must acknowledge the loss and the grief that comes with it.

---

WHAT ARE YOU GRIEVING RIGHT NOW?

HOW DOES THE SPIRIT OF GRIEF SHOW UP FOR YOU?

WHAT HAS IT TAUGHT YOU?

IF GRIEF IS LOVE WITH NO PLACE TO GO, IN WHAT CONTAINER ARE YOU PUTTING YOUR LOVE?

---

## THE DEATH TABOO

Death and dying is one of the world's most consistent promises, yet it is extremely understudied and still quite taboo, particularly in the West.

Death, the permanent ending of a cycle, is a force that changes the lives of the living forever. Losing a loved one reminds us of the sacredness of life and the need to enjoy and experience life fully.

In the midst of writing and attempting to finish this book, the grandmother that I reference quite often throughout this text made her transition into the ancestral realm. What an interesting time she chose to depart. My grandmother Ellestine was an esteemed scholar, homemaker, and most importantly the definition of matriarch. She held God and her family the closest, and made sure to live a life that reflected her love of these things to the highest degree. She is the one who taught me how to cook, but also how to pray. She is the woman who told me that the gift of dreaming was bestowed upon me, and that honoring our ancestral lineage is the key to living a satisfying life. She was a devout Christian with Pentecostal Holiness roots that were nurtured first in the homes of her parents from Manning and Santee, South Carolina. She believed in the power of prayer, singing joyful noises to the Lord, as well as what many would call "superstition." She taught me what to eat on New Year's to ensure prosperity, and that I should not let people roam my house on that first day of the year. She told me not to whistle in the house because it brings misfortune and calls on spirits. She bought me a Voodoo doll when I was a child (I still don't know why) and showed me that you can't hide from people who are connected to Spirit. She encouraged me to listen to what my dreams told me, and encouraged me to "keep going" with my healing work, as I was divinely anointed just like her mother. Although she didn't understand that I was doing these things while not quite identifying as Christian, the Holy Spirit told her that what I was doing was "good," and that was enough for her.

Losing my grandmother, my very best friend, in the midst of writing this book about ancestors was quite an interesting and uncanny experience. As much as I assure people that our loved ones don't "leave us" when they die, that they just transition, I haven't lost anyone as close to me as my grandmother. I now better understand that, in many ways, they do leave us. We learn to love their physical presence—know their scent, admire their voices, and take in their embraces. That feeling has been lost for me, and I can't lie that it's been breaking my heart every single day. Some days I'll just weep, knowing that the saved voicemails I have from her are the closest I'll get to hearing her voice again. It's been really hard. Yet, if I did not have a grounding in ancestral connection and relationship building, I believe that this death would have completely destroyed me. Although I miss her dearly, in my heart I know that she is nearby. In fact, only hours after her funeral, I saw two red cardinals playing and flying right by me! Cardinals are often representatives of transitioned loved ones letting you know that they're okay.

In my dreams I've seen my grandmother, walking down the street of my childhood house in on a beautiful sunny day. I've heard her whispers in my ears and on the wind. I know that I carry her legacy and that I am living testament to *her* prayers. At any point, I can check in with her, ask for a sign, and know that she will always respond. We communicated through dreams while she was alive, and we will continue in the same way. Because of Africana traditions, I can continue to maintain and even build a relationship with her—and all my ancestors—in a way that was not possible while they were living. Humans, although special and multifaceted, have a very limited capacity. Our bodies, although versatile and miraculous, can only do so much while they are living. We can be in only one place at one time, our ability to travel is somewhat limited, and the amount of information that we can retain stops at a certain capacity. Our ancestors, as they transition, are no longer constricted by the body and have a lot more autonomy to live and move freely through the lives of their families and other loved ones. My grandma can be with me and my aunt at the same time. She can hear the things that I may have kept from her while she lived, when I tried to keep her from worrying too much about me. She has been a witness to the mysteries of death and can inform me (as much as my human brain can understand) how to live and love better, as well as how to prepare for the end when it's my time. I encourage us all to learn to embrace death more wholeheartedly, rather than fearing its possibility. Of course it's scary, but our ancestors have managed to do much more in death than many of them could in life. Death can be a blessing.

During my grandmother's eulogy, my cousin Mark—my grandmother's nephew who became a preacher largely because of the spiritual influences of our family—shared three things that my grandma, his Aunt Eila, taught him. The first lesson she taught him was to value lineage. Lineage is, quite simply, your ancestry. It is what you descend from and what descends from you. Your lineage can be understood as exactly what we've been talking about this entire time: acknowledging who you come from, or your ancestors. Lineage involves recognizing the sacrifices of those that came before you, and continuing the legacy of those we revere, as well as knowing that we are never starting from the beginning, nor are we ever alone. Lineage is also recognizing that we can make serious impacts on the worlds around us, and that we will one day be ancestors who have something to contribute and leave for future generations. My grandma always shared stories about our family, as well as life in South Carolina and Baltimore back in the day. The lessons she garnered from her kin are crucial to me.

The next point that my cousin shared was my grandmother's belief in the importance of faith. Faith is the strong belief or confidence in a power. That power for many of my family members is the love of Jesus

Christ, but to me that is the power of the source, our Creator, and the intermediary spirits, including ancestors and Orishas, that are the Creator's hands on earth. Your faith should allow you to feel connected to something powerful and everlasting. Faith should encourage you in moments of sadness and celebrate with you in times of joy. Your faith should bind you to your respective source, and your faith should work for you, not against you. My grandmother was a faithful woman, which is a large part of why I believed she lived the long and successful life that she did. When things didn't go the way she needed them to, she had work and ritual like song and prayer that could shift her situation and bring her peace.

The third point cousin Mark shared was a quote that my grandmother shared often. As a homemaker turned professional woman because she was "tired of being in the house looking at Montgomery Ward department store catalogs," her philosophy was that "as long as you ain't hurting nobody, do what makes you happy!" My grandmommy believed in happiness and doing whatever the hell you wanted! If you want to travel, she felt, then you should travel; if you want to date, then you should date; if you want to go to a concert, then go! She was the queen of following your gut to pursue your wildest dreams. She did not believe in subjecting yourself to unhappiness and doing stuff that did not align with your desires. Although my grandmommy didn't know that I dated women, or identified as a witch (well, she probably did because she was psychic, but I didn't tell her explicitly until her final days), her reiteration of this very quote affirmed that if I was happy she was happy. Of course a big part of this understanding is "as long as you're not hurting nobody..." This aspect of pursuing happiness, I believe, speaks to her understanding of the interconnectedness of people and how our actions can and do impact others. As we pursue our livelihoods, we must be mindful of not subjugating other beings in that pursuit. We have to be careful to not center only ourselves in the journey to living a fulfilling human existence. With that in mind, though, we still have the right to a good life and we should fight fearlessly for our happiness and livelihoods. And trust that she believed in fighting—she was from South Baltimore!

Lineage, faith, and a right to a good life are the tenets that I have kept close to me through the spiritual medicines that have been passed down to me. My ancestors live by these words, and I'm grateful to be able to pull the wisdom from stories such as these, to share with those of you who may need it. Human existence is such a sacred experience, and this iteration of our lives only happens one time. There are so many aspects of our lives that we have control over, and we have a right to grab our life by the reins and steer it in the direction that we desire, with the help of our faith.

# CHAPTER 15

# COMMUNITY (UBUNTU)

Community is a big word in many Africana-rooted spiritual practices and ancestral religions because these practices are all fundamentally community rooted. Embarking upon or continuing this ancestor journey can feel lonely without a community. In ancient times, rituals were done with others. Families were familiar with shrines and took care of them together. Ceremonies and celebrations on behalf of the ancestors and other spirits were normal parts of living and being with one's community. The roles of the ancestors, elders, adults, teens, children, and babies were outlined and respected among groups of people. However, many of us do not live in communal villages anymore. We have been disconnected from our ancestral practices, and perhaps you are the only one in your family or community who believes in ancestral communication and power. Fear not! Believe me when I say that I was the only one who believed it at first, too. Now, seven years after I first constructed mine, my mama has an altar, my bonus father talks to me about Voodoo and his New Orleans roots, and my very Christian grandmother recognized me as a healer. My very Christian friends seek me out for readings and card pullings, and even book healing sessions for their very Christian parents and family members. I promise that the community is there and often in the least expected places. Sometimes the community is right in front of you. Sometimes the community has been waiting on you all along. Allow that to be a possibility, too.

Social media is also such a powerful tool. My very first spiritual community was online! Facebook groups saved me in the first few years of my practice as we discussed rituals, herbs, and other ideas as we studied our ancestral lineages together. I wouldn't be where I am without social media, so do not write it off. Although it is filled with a lot of foolishness, it can connect you to people who are on a similar journey. There are so many ancestor groups these days, I'm overwhelmed. Trust your intuitions about which ones make sense for you, but be open to the magic that does exist in online spaces. The internet is a great resource to find like-minded people. And, as always, ask your ancestors to guide you to the people and places that will support your spiritual growth. Maybe that's your next meditation with them!

Intentional communities are the people whom you choose and who choose you. Every single person is not your community, nor is every family member, online friend, and person who shares facets of your identity. Community, in this context, are the people that value you, work and survive alongside you, support you in your journey (and vice versa). Community are the people whom you intentionally struggle with. Remember that no community is without issues or problems, which is why supporting and valuing each other is an important part of communal values. There are so many differing views regarding ancestors and spiritualities, and many people won't be on the same page. Shit, your ancestors aren't even always on the same page, But that is one of the joys of life: we get to learn and experience the diversity of our lives and thought processes with the other people, the ones we *choose*. Good intentional communities allow you to do that. I often think that we believe communities to be bigger than they actually are. A community can be two or three other people whom we trust and commune with. Be intentional about who those people are and why you consider them to be close connections. Be clear about what kinds of communities you want to be a part of, and those that you want to build. Also recognize your own personal roles in said communities and what strengths and possibly setbacks you offer to a group.

"When the student is ready, the teacher appears" is a quote that I've heard so many times, often when I was completely frustrated that I did not have the elders or in-person community that I wanted. I felt that I was ready, yet I was moving from community to community feeling unsupported, disregarded, and even sometimes disrespected. I needed a teacher or a mentor to guide me through my questions and curiosities to make sure that I was doing my spiritual work correctly. To be fair, I made some mistakes and was unsure, but I continued anyway, being forced to trust my inner voice and the few people I had around me who had sense. I wasn't ready for the direct teacher. I had to have my own core beliefs, my own ancestral relationships, and even my own failures to understand how I would best utilize a teacher. When you are ready, you will have your elder, your high priest, your shamanic guide. When you're ready, it will make itself clear and known to you. Do not give up because you feel like you have more questions than answers—a good spiritual elder will tell you that they do, too.

I think that we are in an interesting time in history because the voice of a true conjure person is being elevated in a way that never has been before. The juju lady, root doctors, and healers have not only been making their presences known but are also actively working to dispel myths and demystify their practices along the way. Yet, even with this unprecedented level of growth and access, finding the kind of healer we need is not always easy. Readers and spiritual practitioners are trying to navigate burnout while not only trying to study the medicine, but often having to sustain other full-time jobs, caring for families, and trying to keep up with being a social media maven. It's a lot.

That is why it is so important to practice patience and kindness toward those who dedicate themselves to helping us on our healing journey. These practitioners should be respected and given compassion. In the old days, the healer was taken care of by the community. In exchange for their work, which brought harmony to the group, they were fed and tended to. If they required a ride, their hair braided, or anything else, those needs would be met with urgency and, most importantly care. But we no longer live in a society that operates primarily from bartering, nor is the healer relied upon in the same ways. Often, seeing a healer is viewed as a quick way to address issues, and so many people question their prices or even these practitioners' desires to earn income in exchange for their services. This is not the way. Healers should be properly compensated for their spiritual work, and their care is a communal responsibility. This lack of reciprocity often leads to burnout. The stresses of daily living can put a damper on all our lives, including the folks who were put on this earth to teach, mentor, and guide us.

Now, more than ever, there are so many people recognizing themselves as healers, yet still there never seems to be enough of them to absolve the worries of the people seeking care. In the same way that hospitals are overflowing, the private messages, emails, texts, and voicemail inboxes of your local juju person are flooded. A fellow practitioner shared the following sentiment with me that changed my entire perspective. I was worried that I wasn't doing enough for the community, and I was swamped trying to get back to people's emails and calls as they agonized over their jobs, their money, their mamas, their men . . . I felt bad that I didn't have a medicine for them on hand, and was so overwhelmed that I started to blame myself. I wondered what would happen if someone lost it all because I wasn't able to be responsive, was too tired, or simply missed their call. A colleague of mine said simply, "People are resilient." This is a simple phrase but one that completely changed my relationship with healing. It was a reminder that what we feel are crises are so often not crises. Yes, there are times when we are in legitimate danger, but so often we may not be—yet our bodies and brains cannot regulate us back to our calm state. We forget to breathe, our minds start racing, our hearts beat faster than normal, and the problem that we are dealing with seems insurmountable. We reach out to someone who can help us in that moment—in my case it was me—and swear that we are in crisis. But we aren't really experiencing a crisis. Nobody has ever reached out to me in a life-or-death situation, probably because I wouldn't be anyone's first point of contact for something so serious, anyway. Yet people have reached out to me with intense urgency, pleading that I respond in that moment to deal with a partner potentially cheating, a loss of a job, or health concerns. All these are topics that one can seek a spiritual practitioner for, but none of these necessitated an immediate response. The fact that people are resilient is not a reason to cast aside their very real concerns, but rather it reminded me—and I hope that it will remind you, the reader—that you have more tools at your disposal than you think. Sometimes the medicine is breathing deeper, and sometimes it is allowing yourself to feel instead of trying to troubleshoot a problem in that very moment. Sometimes it's a nap. I want to empower people to know that the first line of defense when issues arise is *you;* it is not the psychic or the healer. This is a message that I've tried to share within my networks, to remind us that we are resilient, and even though we may feel we need to know something right then and there, often we just need a moment to breathe and think.

CONCLUSION

# SURRENDERING TO SPIRIT

The greatest lesson that will push you as you grow closer to understanding your own spiritual journey through ancestral veneration is the process of *surrendering*. To surrender is to cease resistance, let go, and often submit to some of the circumstances of life. Learning the power of surrendering to Spirit is very important as you delve deeper in understanding more about your destiny. Destinies vary, yet they sketch the loose roadmap of our lives, pointing to the possibilities that exist within our respective realities. Our destiny gives us purpose. It is not a singular path or specific route. The specifics of it can change, but your destiny's energy will likely remain the same throughout your life. You may have a destiny to be a talented musician, as musical abilities run in your family. Whether you become a drummer in an international band or a high school music teacher will be the result of your free will and how you are influenced by different features of your environment, but your connection to music will remain the same no matter what. In order to live our lives with the most dynamic possibilities, we must surrender to the process. This can be one of the hardest things to do when you start intentionally involving your ancestors and Spirit in your life. As humans, we have only a limited understanding of what's possible for us, while our ancestors see beyond that. There are often times when they may push us in a direction that we feel we are not ready for, so we resist the change in order to maintain our own comforts.

In 2018, my ancestors instructed me to leave my work as a full-time organizer-healer in Chicago, Illinois. I was somewhat secure in my position, working alongside people that I respected and even considered friends. In this position, I was able to freely infuse spirituality into our practices as Black organizers in Chicago. However, I started to feel uncomfortable and less sure about my role and what I was doing with my life. Although I was doing honorable work, I felt a tug to move to something more intentional and rooted in my spiritual practices. Of course, as a young adult in a city that's not my home—this absolutely terrified me. "Quit my job and do what?!" was the common question I brought to almost every reading and divination because I knew my ancestors were not actually instructing me to leave my *job*, money, and benefits! Oh, but they were. They ushered me into a role of teaching and studying more about Africana magic and the art of divination. I left my job and my benefits to do just that, and here I am still doing just that. This was my first lesson in surrender.

Our ancestors want the absolute best for us and our lineages. They want to see us thrive and benefit from every opportunity that we can take advantage of while on this earth. I know that I would not have achieved the amount of success and support that I have thus far without the push from my ancestors to surrender what I knew for what I did not know. Who knew that building an altar one day in 2013 would have led me to teaching about the importance of ancestor altars ten years later? I would have never guessed this current trajectory of my life, but my ancestors, Orisha, and other spirits have repeatedly told me that I would have great contributions in spiritual spaces. I had to surrender in order to see that properly.

I have had to let go of lovers, friends, jobs, and beliefs as an act of surrender. So often, our suffering is the result of the painful grip that we have on the things that we know in our hearts are ready to be let go. There is often a perceived peace in the comfort of familiar things—yet there are so many opportunities and blessings in the unknown. Like the Tower card in tarot or the Orisha Oyá of major change, sometimes we have to surrender to "losing" it all in order to gain even more. Because this process is ongoing and difficult, our ancestral support teams can give us the confidence and affirmation we need to make hard choices much more manageable.

You'll have your lessons, too, and they will be hard. Now, I'm not saying go quit your job like I did because your ancestors told you to— but I'm also not saying don't. It made sense for me, and I had to trust that I was a good enough educator and even diviner to devote my life's work to magic. On the surface level, I took quite the risk without a bunch of money in hand, or even a backup plan, but the lesson here is to surrender to what is beyond what you can see. My ancestors were my plans A and B. That may not work for you, but it may. That's up to your path. The humanity in each of us, along with valid reality checks, will try to keep us holding onto security and control no matter what, yet sometimes the lives that we are seeking become present only through the "letting go." By trusting your spirits, your community, and yourself to know that you have achievable visions, you can achieve more than you may realize. It's hard. I still struggle with the process of letting go, and I still experience times where I ignore the advice or pushes I receive from my ancestors, because I want to do what I want to do. I think that's fair as human beings—we are autonomous and are allowed to learn how we want and often need to learn. However, there is so much to say about allowing our ancestral and spiritual faiths to guide us in creating sustainable lives and futures.

Surrendering is not merely letting life happen to you; it is taking ownership of the path you were given, and using the spiritual technologies at hand to alchemize the successes of that path. Surrendering is the acknowledgement of the unknown, and understanding that the only consistent energy we can rely on is change. Change is a natural part of life that cannot be silenced or ignored. The only way to understand and make peace with change is to surrender to the parts that we cannot change, at least not on our own. Make friends with the spirit of surrender and change—it makes for a good offering.

Do not rush your process and own whatever path you decide to take. Your journey is yours, and it is the one that should not be compared with the paths of others. As the Akan proverb goes, "All peppers do not ripen simultaneously." When planting seeds in a garden, all the pepper seeds may not sprout at the same rate. One pepper may grow to its fullest capacity weeks before the other seedlings. This does not make the slower-growing pepper less tasty than the one that was ready to be harvested more quickly. The same can be said for the experience of human beings. We do ourselves a disservice when we assume that because we have not reached westernized versions of "success," we are worthless beings. This could not be farther from the truth. We are all seeds in constant states of growth, seeking water and sunlight one day, ready to be pruned on another. Our ancestors and spiritual allies support our metaphorical gardens by being our very own *Farmers' Almanac*, providing guidance in a world that can feel confusing and lonely. Your desire to connect more deeply with your spiritual senses means that you are in a phase of growth that would welcome the out-of-this-world sense of security and healing that a connection with your ancestors can provide.

My hope is that you use the contents of this book less as a stringent set of rules and more as additional information for your journey. There is medicine within our lineages. There is medicine in the plants outside your home, as well as in the wisdom of an elderly neighbor or your three-year-old baby. Remember that you do not have to be the ultimate practitioner/tarot card reader/psychic medium in order to access the loving embrace of our ancestors. Many of our blessings have already been sacrificed and paid for—we just need to remember them.

My honest prayer is that you allow deep and transformative love to infiltrate your life from across dimensions. May we all remember the prayers that set us free, and may we surrender to the unknown in order to achieve our wildest dreams. May we honor what came before us to inform our next steps. May we collectively engage in practices that resonate with us, and may our ancestors always guide us in a way that supports our fullest potential and destiny.

Thank you for journeying with me, and thank you for answering your ancestral calling with action and intention. Let your ancestors love on you as you enjoy the mysteries, beauty, and exciting complexities of life, and even what comes after that.

# REFERENCES

"Chronology of Catholic Dioceses: The United States of America." *Den Katolsk Kirke*, March 19, 2007, accessed August 23, 2023, https://www.katolsk.no/organisasjon/verden/chronology/usa.

Coffman, Elesha. "A Brief Religious History." *Christianity Today*, January 27, 2010, accessed October 24, 2023, https://www.christianitytoday.com/history/2010/january/haiti-brief-religious-history.html.

Hazzard-Donald, Katrina. *Mojo Workin' : The Old African American Hoodoo System*. Urbana, IL: University of Illinois Press, 2013.

Fraser, Rahim. "Enslaved and Freed African Muslims: Spiritual Wayfarers in the South and Lowcountry: Muslims in West Africa." Lowcountry Digital History Initiative, accessed September 19, 2023, https://ldhi.library.cofc.edu/exhibits/show/african-muslims-in-the-south/muslims-in-west-africa.

Zogbé, Mama. *The Sibyls: The First Prophetess of Mami (Wata): Demystifying the Absence of the African Ancestress as the First Divine Prophetess on Earth*. Martinez, GA: Mami Wata Healers Society of North America Inc., 2007.

# RESOURCES

Here are some books I reference throughout this text that can give you more information about African and African diasporic traditions and religions.

*The Annotated African American Folktales* edited by Henry Louis Gates Jr. and Maria Tatar

*The Black Book* edited by Middleton A. Harris, Morris Levitt, Roger Furman, and Ernest Smith

*Black Magic Religion and the African American Conjuring Tradition* by Yvonne Patricia Chireau

*Fundamentals of the Yorùbá Religion (Òrìṣà Worship)* by Chief Fama

*The Healing Wisdom of Africa: Finding Life Purpose through Nature, Ritual, and Community* by Malidoma Patrice Somé

*The Hoodoo Book of Flowers: The Great Black Book of Generations* by Arthur Flowers

*Hoodoo in America* by Zora Neale Hurston

*Jambalaya: The Natural Woman's Book of Personal Charms and Practical Rituals* by Luisah Teish

*Mules and Men* by Zora Neale Hurston

*The Spirit of Intimacy: Ancient African Teachings in the Ways of Relationships* by Sobonfu Somé

# ACKNOWLEDGMENTS

Many thanks to my God, my ancestors, and my people for uplifting me through every part of this journey. Thank you to the editors and folks at Union Square & Co. for seeing my work and amplifying my words. Big love to my mommy, daddy, DH, and my family for your major support and your sacrifices. Love to my partner for loving me when I prioritized my book over time. Thank you to Arthur Flowers, who lit a fire under my ass to get it done and make it good. Thank you to my spiritual family—from the Hoodoos to those in my ile for your prayers and covering. So much of what I've learned is through being in a community with you. Thank you to my sissy poo, Lyvonne, for showing me what's possible. Thank you to every single person that has ever mentored me, especially to the Black women who saw something in me when I saw nothing.

I extend my love to those who have extended love to me. Thank you so much.

# INDEX

conjurers, 30, 31–32
  High John the Conqueror and, 29–30
  intentions, good/evil and, 28–29
  multiple faith traditions and, 28
  right to freedom, survival and, 27–28
  rituals or "superstitions," 30–31
  "survivor's guilt" and, 27
  Voodoo and, 28
Hygiene. *See* Baths and spiritual hygiene

**I**
Ifa, 16–19
  defined, 17
  destiny and, 23
  history of, 17
  laws, guiding principles, 18–19
  Qrunmila and, 18, 21–22
  roots of, 16–17
  spirits and, 147
  traditional practices, 17–18
  traditional practices (Ifa-Isese, etc.), 17–18
  white baths and, 191–192
Imagination activities, 56–57, 58–59,
    174–175
Incense, on altars, 144
Initiations, 50, 103–104
Intention
  of ancestors, 64–65, 88
  of color incorporations, 198
  in community building, 213–214
  connecting with ancestors and, 39, 59–60,
    111–112, 133, 174–175 (*See also*
    ancestor altars)
  good/evil and, 28–29
  initiation and, 103
  in prayer, 105, 106
Intentional communities, 213–214

**J**
Jakuta, 21
*Jambalaya* (Teish), 142
Journal, ancestral writing ritual, 197–198
Juju
  defined, 11–12
  duality (ancestral understandings) and,
    12, 92
  Juju Bae's name and, 11–13 (*See also*
    Ancestors of Juju)
  magic, witches and, 11–12

**K**
Kids, desire to have, 163–164
Knives, as offerings, 147–148

**L**
LGBTQ, ancestors and, 162–166
Libations, at altar, 149
*A Little Juju Podcast*, 10
"Lost in the spirit" (possession), 132–133
Louverture, Toussant, 123
Love, grief and, 205–206
Luck, ancestral veneration and, 53–54

**M**
Machetes, as offerings, 147–148
Masturbation, 3, 7
McKnight, Jeremie, 119
Mediumship. *See also* Ancestral communication
  about, 131
  claircognizance and, 128
  clairvoyance and, 127–128
Merliza, 30
Money. *See* Prosperity rituals
Moore, Dr., 37, 38
Morrison, Toni, 69, 70
"Mounting" (possession), 132–133

**N**
Natural rituals, 184–189. *See also* Baths and
    spiritual hygiene; Water
  about: connecting with, 185–189, 203
  breathing ritual and, 183–184
  fruit cleansing ritual, 194–195
  grief ritual (connecting with nature), 203
  grounding ritual and, 184
  plant medicine and, 91, 205
Nature. *See also* Animals and animism
  general ancestral spirits and, 71–72
  veneration of, 90–91
Nzinga, Queen of Ndongo, 81

**O**
Obatalá, 20
Offerings, 100–103. *See also*
    Prayer(s); Sacrifices
  altar offerings, 146–148, 150–151
  for ancestral elevation, 204
  coffee or tea as, 148
  defined, 100
  examples, 101–102, 103
  food as, 130, 146–147
  for healing family lines, 156, 181, 182,
    187, 197
  items from earth "marketplace," 102
  knives/machetes as, 147–148
  money as, 197
  purpose and benefits, 101, 121

# ABOUT THE AUTHOR

Kennedi Carter

**Juju Bae** is a practitioner of multiple West African and diasporic traditions, including Ifa and Hoodoo Conjure, and is an Ọṣun priestess within the Orisha tradition. She is the founder of Juju Bae, a multimedia Black-centric resource that seeks to demystify the Black occult through storytelling interviews and lighthearted conversations with twenty-first-century relevance. She is the host of the acclaimed *A Little Juju Podcast*, which encourages Black people to find a home in Africana spiritual spaces and thought, and has starred in the Hulu docuseries *Living for the Dead*. She helps people, young and old, to remember that we have the tools and guidance with us as we journey through this lifetime. Juju is a sought-after spiritual teacher who loves to sing and holds a BA in psychology from Spelman College.